Lemon Drops
A Bittersweet Memoir

FRANCES CHIN

To John,
Thank you for your support.
Enjoy the read!
Gratefully,
Frances Chin

Andrew Benzie Books
Orinda, California

Published by Andrew Benzie Books
www.andrewbenziebooks.com

Some of the names in this book have been changed to protect the privacy of the individuals involved.

Printed in the United States of America

First Edition: March 2015

10 9 8 7 6 5 4 3 2 1

Chin, Frances
Lemon Drops: A Bittersweet Memoir

ISBN: 978-1-941713-05-1

Poems (page 70, 141, 174, 202, 212)
written by Frances Chin, copyright 2015
Cover photo colored by Stanley Chin
Cover and book design by Andrew Benzie

To my husband Stanley Gim Chin—
energetic, gregarious, generous, caring, and solid as a rock
for over fifty years.

To my grandchildren, David, Nicole, Amy and Chloe—
whom we dearly love and who I hope will have as bright a
future as I am enjoying right now.

To my mother, Susie Oy Lum Fong—
who loved lemon drops as much as I did.

CONTENTS

ACKNOWLEDGMENTS

My gratitude to the following:

John Timpane, Media Writer/Editor for the *Philadelphia Inquirer*, who was my "homeroom" teacher at the 2004 Maui Writers Conference and who said, "…the more you polish, the brighter it will shine."

Kayo Hagelin, first person I was willing to let read and critique my early manuscript.

Keith Wong, whom I knew as Feegat and who said after reading my manuscript… "There, indeed, is a pot of lemon drops at the end of the rainbow."

Dr. Samuel Liu, cancer surgeon who said to me, "You are tough!"

Lena Dame, my neighbor in Brentwood, who said I had harbored secrets that scream to be shared, and who believed so much in my writing she was willing to drive me to see a publisher in San Francisco.

And to countless others along the way who influenced and inspired me to forge on, no matter what.

CHAPTER ONE:

ASK ALL YOU CAN

In 1994, when I told Mom I was writing a book (she was 84 years old at the time) and needed her help, she agreed and seemed unafraid to share her personal history. I was thrilled, since her past was not something I was always interested in—until now—and here I was in my 50s. She even reminded me that time was getting short. The first time I asked her about the past, it was over the telephone. When her voice started to quiver, I asked if she was okay, and she said she was. But in the next second, she hung up. Mom was not okay. Whenever her eyes welled up with tears during our face-to-face sessions, I took that as a sign to slow down or back off. Our talks made her assess her life and confront what my dad did and did not do for her or for his children. At the same time, they made me realize what Mom did for us.

We spent many hours talking in her one-bedroom apartment on the ninth floor of the Rose of Sharon Senior Homes on Lakeshore Avenue, Oakland, California, where sunlight beamed in from the west through her sliding glass doors, providing Mom a beautiful view of the rooftops of East Oakland and the City of Alameda across the estuary. She chose that unit because it is on the brighter side of the building at the end of each day, and has a balcony where she maintains a row of potted plants. She moved there when construction of the building was completed in 1976, making her one of the oldest residents and the longest in number of years living there.

It seemed not that long ago that she was independent enough to venture out every day by bus to Oakland's Chinatown to shop and pick up a daily Chinese newspaper. She ate wedges of fresh oranges and did her Tai Chi every morning, but now she is frailer than ever. She should be using a cane or the walker that sits idle in her bedroom, but she refuses. Arthritis, which has caused the knuckles of her fingers to turn white and bulge so that she can no longer wear her cherished rings, occasionally flares up, but she does not complain. At 5 feet 1 inch tall, and weighing 105 pounds, she seemed much taller to me when I was growing up. Now, standing next to her, I seem to tower over her.

Mom tugged at one of the two long white cords dangling behind her tall leather chair and opened the tan-colored, heavily lined drapes that covered the sliding glass door at one end of her living room.

"*Lieng Mah*—Aren't my flowers beautiful?" she asked in Chinese. Mom was proud of her fuchsia pink orchids in full bloom this year, and she wanted a photograph of them. I rolled an old orange swivel chair close to her three potted plants that were sitting on the brown wooden end table. It was draped with a white tablecloth she had embroidered with blue cross-stitch many years ago. I told her to take a seat, and hoped the natural light on her face turned out at least one good photograph. To make sure, I would take a couple of shots using the flash. This time I wanted a picture of her before she asked to be in it, especially since she had turned 93 a couple of months ago. She liked to be in pictures.

"Wait one minute," said Mom, this time in broken English, just before I pushed down the shutter of my digital camera. She got up very slowly and shuffled in calculated steps into the bathroom that adjoined her bedroom.

From the corner of my eye, I saw her look into the metal-framed mirror. The lower part of the mirror was a narrow cabinet for medicine and cosmetics, with two sliding translucent glass doors. In here, Mom keeps a stock of outdated bottles of liquid foundation and a jar of Pond's cold cream on the shelf. She patted her short, once salt-and-pepper, curly permed hair into place, and returned wearing bright ruby-red lipstick and a pair of dangling iridescent opal earrings.

"C'mon, Mom, smile!" Flash. Flash. "One more time… now hold it." Flash.

A week later, I showed her color copies of her various poses, which I printed using my home-computer software. She liked what she saw, including those in wallet sizes. "I am happy," she said in Chinese, "that I was wearing my pink blouse printed with the fuchsia color flowers. It was a perfect match with my orchids." I left extra prints on her small dinette table for my sisters, Marilyn from Orinda and Vickie from San Francisco, for the next time they dropped by to visit Mom. My other two sisters, Joanne, living in Pittsburgh, Pennsylvania, and Muriel, in the Foreign Service in Tegucigalpa, Honduras, would receive their pictures in the mail.

In a corner by the sliding glass door, Mom sat down in her brown leather wingback chair, decorated with curved rows of round brass tacks. I took my usual seat in the center of the queen-size sofa bed, which was covered by a two-tone sage green tapestry cover fringed at the hem, and six decorator pillows in matching shades of green. It reminded me of the times we sat like this as she told me about her childhood, my childhood and my dad. It reminded me of how she sat up, then turned and spoke directly into my cassette recorder, unafraid to share her personal history with me.

As Flo Oy Wong, an artist, a writer and a friend I knew in college, said, "Be glad your mom is around to talk to you. Many of us are not that lucky. Ask her all you can." I did, and it made me realize what Mom did for us.

My mother, Susie Oy Lum Fong, was born, according to the Chinese Lunar calendar, on the 4th month and 14th day of

1910. She lived with her parents, a younger sister, several uncles, aunts and cousins in a large brick compound, along with my great-grandfather (my *Tai Goong*), Lum Hung Sun, the patriarch of the family. He was a Peking scholar from On Tong Village—one of the Loong Du-speaking townships in the Heung San District of Southern China, close to Hong Kong and the South China Sea. Having passed the stringent classical exams required to be a civil service employee, he worked as governor of the county in the nearby city of Shekki. Like members of his family, he often dressed in beautiful silks, satins and brocades.

Great-grandfather had three sons (my grandfather *Lum So Chun* was the eldest) and a daughter (my great-aunt *Goo Por*). There were also two male servants, two maids and a female cook living in the household. One of the servants, *Ah Pong*, carried Mom as a child after school to buy treats down the street, and often she would purchase three bananas for one cent and share them with two cousins. Mom recalls the time she went with *Ah Pong* for a walk in their beautiful garden, when their pet monkey, loose from his chain, jumped on her shoulder and bit the left side of her forehead. To save her life, they captured and killed the monkey, using its gall bladder to brew medicine, which she drank in order to kill the poison in her body.

In 1919, while great-grandfather was away in Shekki, bands of thieves besieged On Tong Village. They relentlessly ransacked his house and stole the family's money and valuables, returning several times that day to continue the looting. My grandfather saved his own life by hiding in a large sewer pipe out in the fields. The women and children ran and hid in a nearby house in the compound, escaping harm. According to Mom, my grandfather studied military tactics at the military academy in Japan when he was fourteen years old, graduating when he was eighteen. Mom was nine when my grandmother, who was seven months pregnant, died at age 30. One year later, grandfather married a Chinese doctor, but Mom's stepmother was not in good health and died four years later, most likely from smoking opium.

In 1926, at age 36, grandfather died, leaving sixteen-year-old Mom and her ten-year-old sister in the care of great-grandfather. Mom loved and respected him. He was big and handsome and looked distinguished, with a full head of thick, black hair, a high forehead and strong facial features complementing his neatly trimmed mustache and goatee. His skin was smooth, compared to the wrinkled skin of the peasants who toiled in the fields and rice paddies that he owned. In family portraits, he postured himself in the center of the group like an aristocrat, but he was kind, wise and protective.

At that time, girls as young as four in China were forced to have their feet bound as a symbol of status and beauty. Their small toes were bent, broken and taped under each foot for years until their feet were permanently disfigured to a point, distorting the bone structure of their feet and stunting their growth to, ideally, only three inches long. As a result, many could not walk and remained in bed or had to be carried everywhere. A few managed to balance themselves and walk by shuffling their bound feet and taking tiny steps, or they ended up crawling on their knees. They literally could never run away. Many died from infection and gangrene, even though their bandages were changed daily, only to be rewrapped tighter. To me, these females in China were used like objects of art on display–suppressed, enslaved and imprisoned by the dominant male society. This practice was done not only by the elite and wealthy but by the lower classes to gain their daughter's desirability for marriage. Great-grandfather eventually disallowed this practice in his house, so my mother and her sister were spared this painful and atrocious custom, which was not outlawed until 1949.

From the time Mom was six, she learned reading and writing in classical Chinese from one of her uncles who taught nearby, and from tutors who came to the house. She was a diligent student and took her schooling seriously, even after her parents died. She also spent time with a next-door neighbor who preached Christianity; Mom then became a believer in God.

Mom, now a young woman, expressed to great-grandfather one day that she wanted to go to Hong Kong to resume her schooling. Great-grandfather responded, "*Oy* (a pet name he gave her, meaning "love"), I already have plans for you. My concern now is to find you a husband. Two years ago, I turned away two possible suitors—one from a nearby village and the other a merchant from America. At that time I thought you were too young to marry. You are now eighteen years old. Your aunt lives in America with her husband, who is doing quite well as an herbalist. I trust she can find you someone to marry in America."

Mom thought it over. Every time her aunt returned home from America, Mom admired the way she dressed in feminine blouses, short skirts, nylon stockings, high-heeled shoes and fur-collared coats. Unlike other Chinese women, Mom was already copying the Western-style hairdo, parting her short black hair into wavy curls and bangs. Mom also envied her aunt's young daughter, cousin Bessie, who wore pretty dresses and pleated skirts, knee-high socks and black leather shoes. Even her aunt's husband, Uncle Shew, was dapper in his custom-tailored three-piece suits, button-down shirts, neckties, two-tone Oxford shoes and argyle socks. In contrast, men in China wore long skirts, quilted jackets with Mandarin collars and cloth slippers. Mom agreed that maybe it would not be a bad idea to marry someone like a businessman from *Gum San*—Gold Mountain "America," which would be better than staying in China. In China, the political climate in the late 1920s with Japan was uncertain and also there was increasing fear of Communism taking over China. Also, Mom heard that girls were not highly regarded or wanted; and "being fed to the pigs" was what happened to Chinese girls. Mom did not like that.

In short order, great-grandfather received a letter from Mom's aunt in America with an 8"x10" sepiatone portrait of a 28-year-old man dressed in a suit and tie, recommending Mr.

Fong Mon Dai, originally from nearby Ho Chung Village, for Mom to marry. He was employed at Uncle Shew's herb store in Oakland, California; great-grandfather agreed with the match. That was in 1928. What Mom and great-grandfather did not know was that Mr. Fong was ten years older than his photograph, and that he had entered San Francisco illegally as a stowaway. Because of the Chinese Exclusion Act of 1900, men who left China to work in America could not bring their wives or children; thus it was common for family members to buy papers declaring to be children of U. S. natives and enter America with false identities and fake names. Mr. Fong and Mom corresponded for years while she waited patiently for him to send for her. During this period, she convinced great-grandfather to provide her with capital to open a small textile business in Hong Kong with a cousin. Within a year, the business failed, and she went back to school in China.

In 1934, much to her dismay, Mom received a letter from Mr. Fong saying he had changed his mind about marrying her and she was free do whatever she wished. She was hurt, then angry! This was not right! She had already waited six years, so she wrote a scathing letter back to him: "I respect whatever you wish, but when you come back to China, please walk on my grave and place a white flower on it." When he showed her letter to two of his relatives, they interpreted it as a threat of suicide (Mom told me she had never contemplated such a thing).

Immediately Mr. Fong bought a set of immigration papers from Mr. Wan, the father of these relatives, for $300, which he negotiated down from $600. He then sent the papers to great-grandfather, who paid for Mom's $300 ship passage… he knew not about the letter of rejection from Mr. Fong to his granddaughter. Upon receiving the set of papers, great-grandfather said to my mom, "You are now twenty-five years old. It will not be easy. You must claim to be the daughter of Mr. Wan. He has six sons, all in America, and one middle daughter, Susie, now married and who wants to remain in Hong Kong. You will be questioned about this family in detail and everything about Susie; you will assume her identity and her name, Susie Fong, and from now on your birthday is May 22, 1910, not April 14. Her six brothers will become your "brothers." Remember, one wrong answer and you will be deported. The interrogators will try to trick you. Never admit that you are going to America to marry, or you will be disqualified, because these papers have no connection to Mr. Fong. Do you understand?" Mom nodded, as brave, obedient and determined as ever.

Great-grandfather placed a two-inch-thick stack of documents in front of her to study—all the facts about the real Susie Fong, written in Chinese by one of her six "brothers" in America. Mom had two months to memorize every detail.

On February 23, 1935, Mom boarded from the docks of Hong Kong the U.S.S. President Coolidge, one of the Robert Dollar steamships, as a third-class passenger. She was confined to her deck and was not permitted to mix with the first- or second-class passengers on the upper floors. The liner made a one-hour stop in Shanghai, where great-grandfather had made arrangements for a driver to take Mom to a hotel to visit with two uncles who were living and working in Shanghai. But one uncle was delayed in meeting her. When Mom rushed back to port to catch the Coolidge, which was still anchored out at sea, the passengers on the last tender had already boarded and the gangplank was raised. Mom was horrified, realizing all her possessions and money were on the ship, but she did not panic. She convinced the oarsman of a rowboat to take her out to the Coolidge before it set sail. When the small boat approached the liner, the crew threw a rope ladder over the side, and as the flimsy "Jacob's Ladder" dangled and swayed from side to side, Mom, wearing a *Cheong Sam* (Chinese long dress), a sweater she hand-knitted, and three-inch high heels, grabbed both ropes of the ladder and climbed to the top, stepping on one rung after another.

All she remembered was shivering, looking straight up the sides of the ship, which was several stories tall, and passing a row of windows before two sailors leaned over the sides to grab her arms and pull her aboard. She thanked God for keeping her from falling into the frigid, choppy waters, and realized there was a reason her *Cheong Sam* had those long slits up the sides! Thank God! She rushed back to her room before anyone reported her missing. Finally, Susie Fong was on her way to America to fulfill her promise, and her dreams of a new life.

Mom shared her cabin on the U.S.S. Coolidge with three other ladies, taking one of the two lower berths. Once a day the porter brought a bowl of water for cleaning up and sponge baths. Mom did not perspire, so she stayed relatively clean. When the seas were extraordinarily rough, Mom would make her way to the toilets down the hall by hanging on to the side rails to keep from being tossed from side to side. She was lucky she never got seasick. All her meals were delivered to her room. When the ship made a stop in Hawaii, two of her roommates disembarked for their final destination. Mom remained on-board this time.

Will I remember all the facts about Susie Fong, the woman I claim to be? If I say the wrong things, will I be booted back to China, and bring shame to my family? People will talk.. Now that I know Mr. Fong does not want to marry me, am I foolish in coming to America? What is America like? They speak a language I do not know. Will I recognize Mr. Fong or any of my "brothers" when they come to meet me? Mom had a lot on her mind.

Upon arrival at the Port of San Francisco on March 13, 1935, after nearly twenty-one days at sea, all immigrant travelers immediately boarded ferry boats for the one-hour ride to Angel Island for screening and clearance. Mom's straight, black hair was matted against her face, the lids of her large brown eyes drooped and her beautiful, white *Cheong Sam* was wrinkled. She hoped to set foot soon in San Francisco, but first she must attend a hearing, scheduled twelve days later on March 25, to testify that she was indeed the alleged daughter of a native. Detainees with the proper immigration papers, like Mom's pregnant friend and her young son Sam, departed to San Francisco with very little delay.

The officials placed Mom with other women detainees in one of the former Army barracks on the island. Women, along with girls, young children and babies, were separated from the men and boys and not allowed to contact each other. When Mom arrived on the island, she placed her large metal trunk in storage. Inside it was a comforter with a beautiful blue satin cover she had designed and embroidered with dragons, birds, flowers and butterflies, along with a pair of matching pillowcases, all for her anticipated marriage. She carried a pair of red slippers she had embroidered, a gas lamp, a large square metal can with preserved food, and a small leather suitcase with a change of clothes up to her room. Her precious jade and gold pieces of jewelry, many given to her as departing gifts, were securely pinned inside a small pocket in the one dress she wore and never took off. Only her underwear was routinely changed and hand-washed. Mom chose a lower cot alongside another lady's cot; each metal bunk had a thin mattress with an army blanket. Since the barracks were not full at that time, many of the upper bunks were dismantled. Her bunkmate cried continually, kept her distance and said very little, but her behavior did not bother Mom.

A stern female guard with even less to say stood duty in the room at all times. At meal-time, a different guard entered and announced, "Chow Chow," then accompanied the ladies to the mess hall, where they sat on benches alongside 12-foot-long wooden tables with stacks of rice bowls and a pile of chopsticks. One scoop of plain rice porridge was served for breakfast, plain rice at noon. For dinner, the detainees served themselves from large aluminum bowls of rice, with simple vegetables like Napa cabbage and *Chinese bok choi.* Mom ate very little, but for her it was enough. One detainee's husband, owner of the Lun Kee Restaurant in Oakland, prepared roast pork and soy sauce chicken and delivered them by ferry to his wife. She befriended Mom and often shared these dishes with her and the other detainees.

Mom found little to do at Angel Island. At night she heard screams and cries from women who could not take the wait or were being deported back to China. She heard stories of many who had committed suicide or tried to stop breathing by sticking their heads into the toilets because they would rather die than be held prisoner in a country they had thought stood for liberty. Three times a week, the guards led the detainees across the yard, where they spent half an hour gazing across the waters toward San Francisco, where Mom dreamt one day she would step ashore. Mom enjoyed the fresh air and the wind on her face. Once a week a nun called "Mama" came with knitting yarn and embroidery thread to teach small handcraft projects, the only time some of the women perked up. To pass the time, Mom read poems penned on the walls about sadness, despair and giving up. The guards often taunted the women by saying, "You go back to China," bringing some of them to tears. Mom had no idea what those words meant until she learned some English words a few years later. Missing their homeland and wanting to return, many women wondered why they ever came. Others remained hopeful… Mom was one of them.

On March 25, 1935 (two weeks after her arrival on Angel Island), Mom appeared before the Board of Special Inquiry. The Board consisted of two Federal inspectors, a stenographer to record the testimony and an interpreter. Simultaneously, in another room, two of her "brothers" from San Francisco were questioned as to the facts of their family. Mom's answers would have to agree with their statements or deportation back to China was sure. Mom, with her independent mind and spunky spirit, waived the right to have a relative or friend present during the hearings, and elected to answer all questions on her own. This, according to a transcript obtained in the 1980s by my sister Muriel from the National Archives Records Administration (NARA) Pacific Region in San Bruno, was literally part of the actual questioning:

Question: What are all your names?
Answer: Fong Susie; no other.
Question: What is your natural dialect?
Answer: Heung Shan.
Question: Is that the dialect in which you will testify?
Answer: Yes.
Question: You are also informed that the burden of proof rests upon you to establish your right to admission to the United States. Do you understand?
Answer: Yes.
Question: By reason of what facts do you consider yourself admissible to the United States?
Answer: Because my father was a native-born citizen of this country.
Question: Who is your father?
Answer: Fong Wan; Fong Jeung Wun.

The questioning continued into the third and final day, with the heaviest and most detailed on the last day. There were questions regarding relatives and neighbors, her six brothers, and their families, questions about her village, the distance in feet to the rice fields and to the house next door, her bob haircut, and a full description of the house she lived in:

Question: Describe the interior arrangement of your house.
Answer: On the ground floor as you enter from the front door there is a parlor, then a bedroom next to the parlor. There is a hallway next to the bedroom on the south side of the house—this hall leads from the front parlor to the second parlor; there is another bedroom next to the second parlor, with a kitchen at the rear; over the second parlor there is an upstairs, which has two bedrooms; there is a back door opening from the kitchen at the rear.

There were questions about who slept in each bedroom; her schooling at the Fong Village Ancestral Hall: its location, the classroom, the furnishings, where she sat, and the names of her teacher and classmates; her job as a sewing apprentice in Hong Kong, and much more. The inspectors showed her a number of photographs of each of her six brothers to identify. She identified four of them, but failed to recognize the other two. The hearing was over, and she would have to wait for their decision.

On March 29, 1935, Edward L. Hafp, Director of the San Francisco District No. 19 of the Immigration and Naturalization Service of the U.S. Department of Labor, sent a letter to Mom's American attorney, W. G. Becktell. It stated that her application had been denied on the grounds that she failed to sustain the burden of proof, but she had five days to appeal the decision. Mr. Becktell immediately contacted two of her brothers, and, through their testimony and insistence that she was their sister, she was released after nearly two months of detention. Her brothers paid Mr. Becktell $300 for representing her case.

When the guards in the barracks called out her name, SUSIE FONG, to announce her departure, the remaining detainees knew she was free to leave. She gathered her things, but felt bad for those she was leaving behind. She left her red embroidered slippers to one of the ladies who admired them and boarded the ferry to meet the stranger she was to marry.

In 1985, my mother wrote this poem in Chinese, which was later translated into English:

> Fifty years ago—locked up in this building
> After three days' interrogation,
> The punishment was deportation.
>
> Every day I cried for fear of going back.
> Every night I am uneasy as I hear
> The waves crash angrily.

Mom did not cry every day as her poem suggested, but she did fear the worst possible outcome being deported back to China. Her writing was undoubtedly influenced by the poems she read on the walls at Angel Island. I continued to ask my questions and Mom told me more...

CHAPTER TWO:

MARRIAGE TO A STRANGER

When Mom set foot in San Francisco in March 1935, two of her so-called brothers were there to greet her; a cousin was the driver. For now, Mom was to stay with him and his wife in their apartment at Chinatown by the Broadway Tunnel. Neither Mr. Fong Mon Dai (also known as Diamond Fong, her appointed husband) nor Mom's aunt were there to welcome her because they feared she could be followed by immigration officers. If she was caught in the company of her real relatives after leaving Angel Island, Mom would undoubtedly be arrested for lying to the officials.

For several days, two or three of her brothers at a time took her dancing and out to dinner and to see Chinese movies and live operas; afterwards they would all have a late evening snack at the Sun Hung Heung Restaurant on Washington Street. Mom, age 25 and young at heart in a new country, enjoyed wearing the Western-style dresses and fur-collared coats she borrowed… and the lavish attention from the men. However, when Mr. Fong came to visit, he was quiet and said very little to her. One time, Mom was instructed to meet Mr. Fong at a motel, and although he took an adjoining room, he did not see or speak with her that night. Early the next morning, he disappeared for work without saying a word of goodbye.

Mom continued to stay with different relatives. About two or three weeks after her arrival in San Francisco, afraid that Mom was having too good a time, her aunt *Goo Por* came with a relative who had a key to Mr. Fong's apartment. On their way toward Grant Avenue and Sacramento Street, Mom heard the clacking and "washing," or shuffling, of *Mah Jong* tiles from a game similar to the gin rummy the Chinese people love to play. Those familiar sounds of people playing *Mah Jong* resonated from the open windows of the tall apartment buildings as well as from the open steel trap doors on the sidewalks, used during the daytime hours to lower deliveries to the basements. Mom and her aunt forged ahead and entered the four-story Nanking Building at 825 Sacramento Street, one of many buildings owned by businessman Joe Shoong. Next door was the YMCA, and across the street, on the corner of Waverly Place, was the Salvation Army Building. On another corner was the Chinese Baptist Church, a brown brick building built in 1888 and rebuilt in 1909 after the Great Earthquake; adjacent to the church was the Chinese Community Playground. Mom entered Apartment #303 on the third floor and was left there to familiarize herself with Mr. Fong's one-room apartment and small kitchen.

Four small communal bathrooms were down the hall. The one closest to their apartment had a single bathtub that was shared by other residents on the floor while the other three bathrooms each had a toilet. The bathrooms were dirty and smelly, and Mom was afraid to use them. Instead, in the apartment she used a Chinese porcelain vase that was slightly taller than a spittoon bowl, and each day emptied the contents into one of the toilets. At the end of the hall was a room with a special chute for disposing of garbage and trash.

Mr. Fong looked not much older than his portrait. At 5 foot, 6 inches and weighing 135 pounds, he appeared slender and tall, compared to her 5 foot, 2 inch height. He wore a three-piece suit with a pocket watch dangling from a long gold chain, and carried a hat.

Immediately, Mom asked a resident in the building, Mrs. Low on the fourth floor, to teach her how to use a sewing machine, something she had started to learn from her first place of stay. Mom learned quickly and found work sewing nurses' uniforms at the sewing factory on the ground floor of her apartment building. Upon her insistence, Mr. Fong spent $60 for a commercial heavy-duty Singer treadle sewing machine so she could sew at home too. Then she went to work at the National Dollar Store, also owned by Mr. Shoong, earning $12 per week sewing, to supplement Mr. Fong's sporadic weekly earnings of $9 as a kitchen helper.

Pregnant in June with their first child, on November 16, 1935, Mom went to the Superior Court of San Francisco to legalize their marriage. Judge Edmund P. Mogan officiated, with two of Mr. Fong's friends from San Francisco, Frank L. Chinn and William J. Chow, witnessing the simple ceremony. When Judge Mogan asked Mr. Fong for the wedding ring, he did not have one, much to Mom's disappointment. Mom glanced at the pearl-and-jade stone ring she was wearing, which she brought from China. She reversed the ring and used the bottom of it on top, as her wedding band. The marriage license stated she was 24 and he was 38, but those were not their true ages. On that day, she became Mrs. Diamond Fong, fulfilling the promise she made in China seven years ago to marry him.

From this point on I refer to Mr. Fong as my father. I have a harder time calling him Dad, but sometimes I do.

On March 12, 1936, Mom gave birth to their first child, Marilyn, at the Chinese Hospital on Jackson Street. Mom also gave her a Chinese name, *York Chee*, meaning Nice Personality. The three of them moved into Apartment #304, a larger unit across the hall, with a kitchen to the right of the living room and a separate bedroom to the left. Rent was now $16 a month… well worth the extra $4. Two of the four burners on the old stove did not work, and frying smoked up the kitchen. With the help of a friend, my father installed a portable, three-burner gas cooking unit on a shelf he built outside the window by the old stove. Mom never cooked on the new burners because she could not reach that far, to open or close the window. When I asked her what happened to the stove when it rained, she did not recall!

Less than two years later, on January 26, 1938, Mom gave birth to her second daughter, Joanne, giving her the Chinese name *York Gnaan*, meaning Pretty. I was born on March 27, 1939, the Year of the Rabbit according to the Chinese Lunar Calendar, weighing 6 pounds 8 ounces, the smallest and tiniest of all her babies. One year later, Muriel arrived on Mom's Chinese birthday, April 14. My Chinese name is *York Ping*, and Muriel's is *York Teng*. Together *Ping* and *Teng* mean Peaceful and Calm. *York* in all our names means Long Standing and Forever. Except for Marilyn, who was born in a hospital, the rest of us were born at home, in Apartment #304.

Still avoiding the communal bathrooms, Mom, through each pregnancy, climbed into the small concrete washtub next to the kitchen sink for her weekly baths, first stepping on a kitchen stool, then onto a chair to the counter. This was also where she bathed us and washed our hair, assembly-line style, before towel-drying us on the large round wooden kitchen table. Mom arose every morning while the sky was still dark to hand-wash our laundry, then carried several loads of wash two flights upstairs to the roof, to use the clotheslines before other tenants beat her to them. If it rained, we were all out of luck. When Muriel was born, I was barely a year old, Joanne was two and Marilyn just turned four. Although Joanne was potty trained, there were plenty of cloth diapers in the wash between Muriel and me and plenty of work for Mom, who continued sewing and caring for the four of us by herself.

I do not recall my father being around very much in my early childhood, but he must have been, to get Mom pregnant four times within her first five years in America! He did not contribute much to our household or well-being, but he did pay the rent most of the time and always made sure Mom had a sack of rice in the kitchen. When Mom first met him, he was cooking, washing dishes, and brewing herbs in Oakland—far from being a businessman. Later, his odd jobs as a kitchen helper and seasonal worker took him out of town, to work in canneries or pick fruits in small towns like Suisun and Niles.

Occasionally he showed up at home on Saturdays. Those few times were special because he prepared his favorite dish, Chinese braised chicken. It was not the usual pale, tasteless, bloody-at-the-bones steamed chicken. It was not the dark soy sauce chicken that came in a white take-out paper box with the wire handles and red good fortune symbols. It was prepared from freshly butchered chicken that he bought at the Dupont Market, just a few steps down Grant Avenue. That was the street where one year my sisters and I stood on the corner with Mom and watched Madam Chiang Kai-shek from Taiwan, formerly Formosa, ride in a parade soliciting support and donations for her party, the Chinese Nationalists.

Sometimes my dad took me along to buy freshly butchered chicken, and I scurried to keep up with his long strides; I was especially delighted when he, without saying a single word the entire time, took my hand in his. Grant Avenue was crowded with cars parked on both sides. A truck driver slamming the door of his delivery truck startled me, as an ambulance with its sirens blaring raced through the narrow streets. I was not used to the sounds of the outdoors since Mom kept us inside most of the time. I strained to hear the motor of an airplane and stared with squinted eyes until the plane faded into the cloud-filled sky. I looked up at the tall buildings… narrow, cramped, sandwiched between skinny alleys. Some had signs written only in Chinese characters while others had layers of red, orange or green glazed ceramic tiles that formed roof lines into the shape of pagodas. Far East Café was around the corner, while up the street was the Tung Sen Tong Benevolent Association, where my dad was a member, organized as a place to socialize and to help fellow Louie, Fong and Kong clan immigrants settle into their new lives. Like other family associations in Chinatown, members also helped read and write letters to China for those who were not literate.

Nearby was a Chinese herb shop where Mom and Dad bought medicinal tea when one of us was sick. The herbalist would weigh and measure out roots, leaves, bark, beans, pods and powders from narrow, deep drawers along one wall behind the counter, tap the ingredients together into a square piece of paper, fold the ends together like an envelope, and enclose instructions handwritten in Chinese characters. I was fascinated and watched the herbalist calculate the cost on an old abacus, tapping and sliding rows of wooden beads representing digits inside a handheld, toy-looking wooden frame. Each prescription included a small pack of sweet, yellow raisins—my reward if I drank my cup of bitter tea, which was hard to swallow without making a face or wrinkling my nose. For other ailments, I remember swallowing Chinese medicine in the shape of tiny red beads *bo jay een* that came in a small glass cylinder bottle or drinking a dosage of *sup lung don*, a white powder substance dissolved and mixed with water in a Chinese soup spoon.

As my dad and I continued our walk to the poultry shop, I glanced at Eastern Bakery on the corner of Commercial Street, craving one of the small, scallop-shaped sponge cakes, *gay don go,* in the window, but we did not stop. Still not a word from Dad. Inside Dupont Market were cages of squawking chickens stacked to the ceiling. The gray, discolored wooden floor of the market was sprinkled with sawdust, which a worker swept up at the end of each day. A ceiling fan revolved overhead by the entrance, creaking slowly as if the motor would die at any minute. But that fan did not cool the place, keep the flies from coming in, or rid the foul smell in the air.

Dad made his selection by pointing to one of the chickens; the butcher grabbed it by the neck and slit its throat. Blood gushed and splattered. Yuck! The butcher tossed the fighting bird into an empty aluminum garbage can, capped its lid and waited until the thrashing stopped. I jumped at the noise. He then plucked the feathers, using a special machine for the job. As we passed the garbage can I could not help taking a peek at the bloody red mess. The sight made me cringe and shiver. Arriving home with the freshly butchered bird, Dad used garlic, ginger, salt and soy sauce and braised the whole bird in hot sizzling peanut oil to seal in the flavor. The taste of the crispy skin was scrumptious with our bowls of plain steamed rice. What a wonderful treat for us!

Sometimes we would leave the meat market with raw chicken feet wrapped in pink butcher paper. Using special Chinese spices and ingredients, Mom or Dad would stew the raw slippery web-like pieces of chicken feet with the long pointed toe nails until all the meat slid off the bones, and the bones fell apart at the joints. To me, licking and sucking on the bones was as delicious as chewing the meat!

Muriel was Dad's favorite daughter. He considered her his lucky child because she was his fourth-born with a birth date of 4-14-40 (Mom's true birthday was also April 14). Although I was his third-born, I guess three and multiples of three in my birth date did not count. Mom said Muriel was the easygoing one, and I was the crybaby, so Mom had to carry me everywhere. She would tuck me under one arm while she used her free hand to wash, cook with chopsticks, feed my sisters and me and eat her meals, switching arms when she got tired. When Mom sewed, she kept one foot on the pedal while her other foot rolled my stroller back and forth like a rocker to keep me pacified. Marilyn and Joanne played in the living room and kept each other company while Muriel remained docile. I fussed and carried on for hours and sometimes for days.

Once in a long while, my dad would ask me to come and sit by him. I would run over and, with my back to his chest, place my elbows on his knees, dangle my legs and swing back and forth between his legs. I loved it, because Mom rarely let us out to play on the swings at the playground. Sometimes Dad would slip one of his hands under the back of my dress and rub slowly across my back and shoulders. I wanted him to rub longer because the warmth and touch of his large, strong hands made me feel special. Night came and by morning, he would disappear. Mom did not know when he would come home again, but I never missed him.

"Through all this, did you ever cry?" I asked Mom once. "I never saw you cry."

"Yes, you did," said Mom. "One time you witnessed me crying at my sewing machine, toddled over, patted me on the shoulder and told me not to cry. You said, 'Don't worry, Mom. When I grow up, I will take care of you.' You were three years old. I was crying because I noticed some of my jewelry, and money I had earned and placed in a drawer, were missing. I finally realized your father was taking them without my knowledge to repay the debts he owed. One time I confronted him and found he had hocked some of the precious gold jewelry given to me in China: a gold star pin, bracelets, a beautiful opal ring from your great-aunt, and a gold ring that was a baby gift to Marilyn. Luckily I found a claim stub for one of the pieces and was able to buy it back from the pawn shop for ten dollars, paying an additional five dollars to the store-keeper as interest. Another time he wanted to sell my sewing machine, but I would not let him. I was stubborn because that would have stopped my much-needed earnings… earnings I later used to pay people who approached me about his ongoing debts. I never liked confrontation like that. "Ai ya" (which means "Oh, my").

Little did Mom know that her life would be complicated by the outbreak of World War II, but it did not turn out all bad for her.

CHAPTER THREE:
WORLD WAR II YEARS

In the early 1940s, Mom went to work sewing denim jeans at a small factory at the corner of Sacramento and Stockton streets in San Francisco. She also took bundles of material to sew at home and carried armloads of finished garments back up the hill to the shop. Joanne, age five, attended half-day kindergarten at the St. Mary's Chinese Catholic Center on the corner of Stockton and Clay Streets, about a block from Mom's work. Joanne's tuition was based on Mom's low income and the size of our family, so the amount was affordable. When Joanne got off school, Mom took her break and walked a block to meet Joanne at the corner.

"Look both ways for cars before you cross the street," cautioned Mom. "And don't run."

For the rest of the day, Joanne sat and played quietly by Mom's sewing machine, lying down on the floor for a nap when she was tired. Marilyn, nearly seven, was old enough to attend Commodore Stockton Elementary School on Clay Street on her own. Muriel and I were placed conveniently in free nursery school classes at the YMCA, next door to our apartment building. I remember we sat outside at recess time on long wooden benches and heard the Chinese National Anthem blare out of loud speakers while we drank our glasses of sour tomato juice, a taste new to me. Between working and caring for us, Mom had little time to shop for food, but a kind neighbor across the hall who had a telephone allowed Mom to use it. She called a grocer who delivered our orders as he made his daily rounds in our building, charging an additional ten cents for each delivery.

As my sisters and I were growing up, our birthdays were not celebrated with gifts and parties. Apparently in May 1940, a month after Muriel was born, Mom looked forward to celebrating her Chinese thirty-first birthday, which was really her thirtieth, since the Chinese consider a newborn baby, carried nine months in the mother's womb, one year old at birth. Traditionally, Chinese people celebrate "big birthdays," especially for elders on their fifty-first birthdays and every ten years thereafter, by inviting friends and relatives to a fancy Chinese banquet. According to Mom, few people in China reach their 80s, but if any wealthy person in China reached 100, a village gate, or *pi fong*, was erected to honor the celebrant for the rare milestone. Mom described a *pi fong* as similar to the elaborate gate on Grant Avenue and Bush Street welcoming tourists to San Francisco Chinatown. That day in May was very special to Mom, but when my dad was not home to help her celebrate, her eyes welled up with tears. She perked up, however, when a young American-born Chinese lady in Apartment #305 knocked on our door, bringing a tray containing five heaping bowls of cooked food. The neighbor spent $2.90 to have chicken, duck, mixed vegetables, spareribs and a combination dish of fish and tomatoes delivered from a restaurant, but the order was way too much for her and her boyfriend to eat, so she shared the abundance of food with us. Mom thanked God for the miracle and the meal, which lasted us for days.

During this period, Japan was at odds with the United States. On December 7, 1941, the Japanese bombed Pearl Harbor on the Hawaiian Islands, causing the United States to declare war on Japan. Because the Japanese living in America were believed to be threats to our national security and not to be trusted, most lost their homes and businesses and were confined to internment camps throughout the country. In spite of this treatment, when our men and women were called into the Armed Services, many Japanese with U. S. citizenship proudly enlisted in the United States military forces, some later forming the 442nd Battalion. Dad dutifully registered on February 15, 1942, with the Selective Service of the United States and was required by law to carry his registration card at all times.

Jobs became plentiful as women took over work traditionally held by the men who had marched off to war. There were many, like the famed "Rosie the Riveter," who worked in the shipyards and factories to keep the economy going. A neighbor across the hall convinced Mom to leave her sewing job for a higher-paying one at Simmons Mattress Company, which had been converted from manufacturing mattresses to producing items for the war effort. The $42 a week she earned was much more than being paid piecework for the jeans she sewed at her last place of employment. Even Dad found a full-time job in town, as a kitchen helper at the B&K Coffee Shop on Geary Street. According to old copies of my parents' 1040 Income Tax Return (they paid around $7 for a public accountant to prepare them), he made well over $2200 a year during the war years… but Mom saw very little of it. However, he was home every night, which made it possible for Mom to take the night shift from four to midnight, walking nearly twenty blocks along Stockton and Powell Street to Fisherman's Wharf. Joanne and Marilyn were left home alone for about an hour and a half each day until Dad came home at five after picking up Muriel and me from the "Y." Mom took a short break at eight, sometimes eating the dinner she packed, two slices of white bread spread with butter. She had no idea what lunchmeat and mayonnaise were. She also had no idea what Dad was making.

Mom's evening work hours allowed her to attend English classes at the Chinese Presbyterian Church on Stockton Street, where she was baptized within weeks after her arrival in San Francisco. She knew the importance of learning English so that she could one day pass the test to become a naturalized citizen of the United States. She attended Sunday church services there and sometimes took us along, although it was hard for me to understand the sermons that were spoken in a Chinese dialect I did not understand; often I dozed off to sleep.

Since the Simmons Mattress Company was under contract to the federal government, the factory was swarming with military personnel overseeing production. Mom's job was to stamp the glass lens for the rubber gas masks. She sat at a special machine, positioned the round glass pieces exactly over each eye hole of the metal frame, and automatically the machine clamped down on all the layers. If her timing was off and the machine missed its mark, the mask was tossed into the reject pile. Mom rarely missed.

A month after Mom started working there, production shifted to making Army tents with heavy, olive-drab canvas material. Mom sat at a heavy-duty treadle sewing machine, with another sewing machine table butting up right next to hers. Another pair faced the first two and formed one of several work units. Automatic pulleys on cables suspended from the ceiling moved the heavy tents along. Four men working together reached up, yanked the tent down, and positioned a corner onto each of the four sewing tables. Each seamstress sewed a corner as fast and as accurately as possible, clipping the heavy threads just as the same team of men grabbed and guided the tent back up the moving cables to the waiting arms of the next four men in the assembly line.

Though the war created jobs, it also created shortages. By 1942, everyone in the country received war rations. Those books of color-coded stamps allowed the distribution of certain food products and goods: eggs, milk, sugar, oil and nylon stockings. By the time we were issued War Ration Book #4, warnings were issued to "never buy rationed goods without ration stamps" and "never pay more than the legal set price," in an attempt to stop the black market.

Sixty years later, when I questioned Mom about the stamps and showed her my ration book, she said she never saw them and did not know they existed. We surmised together that Dad had signed for our books and had complete control over their use, without Mom's knowledge.

On August 8, 1945, the United States retaliated by bombing Hiroshima, Japan, and on August 9, the target was Nagasaki. Seven days later, the United States was the victor, and when hundreds of employees and military personnel heard the announcement at work, they shouted in celebration. Although Mom did not understand all the commotion, she knew it was good news, and after nearly four years, the war was over.

The Simmons Mattress Company converted back to producing mattresses and retained Mom, one of the best workers, to sew the cording on the padded covers of the box springs. One day she showed up for work but her boss told her she had been laid off, with the promise she would be rehired when work picked up. However, when Simmons did not call her back, she returned to her old sewing job in Chinatown. She wanted to return to work for Joe Shoong, where the money would have been better, but she heard one of his employees was trying to unionize the shop. Mr. Shoong did not want to go through the hassle, so he shut down his sewing business and was not hiring.

While Mom made good money at Simmons, she set aside some of each paycheck to buy U.S. Savings Bonds. It was another way she supported the war effort, and it paid off in more ways than one… and she made enough money to send us to the movies nearly every Sunday.

CHAPTER FOUR:
MISSING MARILYN

On Sundays when Dad was not home, Mom often took us to see Chinese movies. These were contemporary dramas, traditional operas, or stories of warlords fighting neighboring warlords, invaders or foreigners, but I could never understand the stories. The women's roles in the operas were often portrayed by male actors with high-pitched voices, broad sweeping eye-brows, rosy red cheeks, bright red lips and faces made to look like opaque white porcelain skin, a mark of beauty. The actors wore colorful embroidered silk costumes with long, flowing sleeves and elaborate headpieces embellished with sequins, beads, and tassels. Stiff, long flaps in the shape of small ceiling fan blades jutting from the sides of their faces quivered with each animated jerk the singers made while cocking their heads from side to side.

The actors spoke and the singers sang in a classical Cantonese dialect unfamiliar to me. It was not the village Heung San and Shekki dialect Mom taught us to speak. We were supposed to learn Loong Du, my Dad's dialect, but Mom wanted us to speak something more citified and sophisticated. Once in a while I recognized a word or two in the movie, but soon enough my eyelids would close and I would drift off to sleep, like the times I went to church with Mom and could not understand the sermons.

The funniest movies were the ones where Kung Fu fighters somersaulted and back-flipped across the screen, ending up in a single leap on top of fifteen-foot walls like Superman or Batman, except without the capes. Back then, the Chinese were already creating visual effects on film... like Academy Award-winning director-producer Ang Lee did more recently in *Crouching Tiger*. Watching the actors in *Crouching Tiger* chase each other across rooftops, leap, sword-fight and disappear behind treetops brought back fond memories of the old Chinese movies I saw as a child.

As we became older, Mom sent us to the movies by ourselves. There were two theaters in Chinatown, but most often we attended the Great Star Theater on Jackson Street, between Kearney and Grant. "Now, hold each other's hands tight," Mom said. "Watch out for cars. Go directly to the theater. Don't talk to strangers. Don't talk to anyone. There are bad people out there." We went the shortest route, taking Waverly Place or Grant Avenue, crossed Clay and Washington, and cut through alleys to Jackson. "Look both ways for cars before you cross the street," said Marilyn, "Hold hands and don't run." Marilyn, age six, held fourteen cents to buy two tickets—one for herself and one for Joanne. Muriel and I, aged two and three, got in free.

Since Mom did not give us extra money, though she was earning good money during the war, we could not stop at the snack bar in the lobby, but I glanced at the long counters anyway. I was amazed that the glass jars with the round metal lids and red bead on top, tilted at an angle with goodies inside, did not tip over. There were jars of red and black licorice, packs of pink bubble gum, green Doublemint gum, white Spearmint, yellow Juicy Fruit and all flavors of Chiclets—little square pieces of gum with the rounded corners, two in each tiny yellow box. There were sweet and sour preserved fruit, dry salted plums, candied ginger, beef jerky, and bags of roasted peanuts, popcorn and Chinese melon seeds. And packages of yellow lemon drops—my favorite. My mouth watered. I longed for something, anything… but not today.

On one occasion, my sisters and I pushed our way though a set of heavy velvet curtains into the main theater. It was pitch-black. We blinked our eyes and saw the silhouette of four empty seats toward the back of the theater, tip-toed across the row, knocking into a few knees and stepped on melon shells scattered all over the floor, causing us to make crackling noises that annoyed the patrons seated nearby. The Chinese are notorious for cracking melon seeds with their teeth, eating the meat inside, and then spitting the shells on the floor. Someone in the row in front of us turned around and said, "Shhh...Sit down." We finally settled into our seats. Hours after watching two featured films, cartoons and the RKO Newsreel of the Week in black-and-white, we exited the theater into the blinding light.

We continued to take several of these Sunday trips to the theater while Mom stayed home. I wonder what she did while we were at the movies. Maybe she did the ironing, since she always kept us in clean, starched cotton dresses. Anyway, I'd like to think that it was peacefully quiet for her.

On another occasion, after the lights dimmed in the theater, I glanced across the two or three empty seats next to me and saw an old creepy Chinese man trying to catch my attention. In the dark I could see he had a nasty grin from ear to ear on his face. I remembered my mom warning us about talking to strangers. I turned away, curled up in my seat with my knees drawn to my chest, threw my sweater over my face, and fell asleep. When I heard my sisters beckoning me, it was time to head home, and I was safe for now. I did not know what movies played that day and I did not mention a word to anyone, not even to Mom. I knew he was someone scary… and not my imagination.

In spite of the incident, I continued going to the Chinese movies with my sisters, keeping the secret to myself and my mother's words of warning in my head. Muriel remembers the spooky restrooms downstairs and playing in the aisles during the movies. What were once black-and-white films on the silver screens were eventually replaced by cinematography in color on the wide screen, and Mom sent us off to the movies for years to come.

In 1943, when Marilyn was nearly seven years old, she contracted the measles. Mom kept her home for a couple of weeks, but sent her back too soon to Chinese school, where Marilyn caught a cold and became very ill. The doctors diagnosed her with tuberculosis (TB). At that time, there was a serious outbreak of the disease, and in order to stop the spread of TB, anyone having it was quarantined. Representatives from a private care facility (perhaps the one named Hasler's Health Club) in Belmont, a city not far from San Francisco, came and took Marilyn away for treatment. She cried as the car pulled away from our apartment building, thinking she was being given away for good. Mom did not apply for county assistance for fear the agents would find out that she and our father were both here illegally, so she paid one hundred dollars for each of the first three months, but when she exhausted the money she saved from sewing, she appealed to the hospital for help and the administrators waived all future payments for Marilyn's care. Mom went weekly by bus to Belmont to visit Marilyn; Dad sometimes accompanied her. Joanne, Muriel and I were too young to understand what was going on and probably did not miss her. Anyway, Marilyn was no longer responsible for taking us to the movies.

One time while Marilyn was confined in Belmont, Mom ran out of material from the factory to sew at home. She told the three of us, "I have to go out for a short while. Chain and lock the door after I leave and don't let anyone in. Watch one another. Stay inside the apartment." She left, and I could hear the clicks of her heels fade down the hall. As instructed, we locked the door and latched the chain. Joanne, five years old, I at four and Muriel at three were left alone. We heard children playing out in the hall and it sounded like they were having fun running, laughing and chasing. Some were racing up and down the stairwell just outside our door. We wanted to join our friends, so we looked at each other contemplating what to do.

"But Mommie told us not to," whimpered Muriel. "She'll get mad at us."

"No, she won't," stammered Joanne. "We'll go quickly and be right back. We promise. Mommie won't know." I looked at Joanne in agreement. *No, Mommie won't know.*

We unchained the door and stepped out into the hall. Down the hall lived Benjamin Tong and his brother, and Steve Wong and his family. On the fourth floor lived Mrs. Low, the one who taught Mom how to sew. She wore her short hair in tight pincurls and lovely Chinese dresses instead of Western-style clothes, and she had eight children. Close to our ages were Nancy, Emily, Maxine and Victor. Mom had the honor of giving Victor his Chinese name, *Teen Chee* (gift from God), when he was born. His four older sisters were Bessie, Edna, Pearl and Ruby. The latter two took Mom shopping when she needed something from downtown. When Mom took Marilyn and Joanne out, or sometimes Muriel and me, she relied on Mrs. Low to babysit the two who were left behind. I remember those times, lying down for a nap on their lumpy brown leather sofa in the kitchen and staring at the big ugly cockroaches on the wall. I watched them scurry sideways up toward the ceiling going nowhere and falling behind the sofa to the floor, still going nowhere.

I think of the many times during the middle of the night I felt the legs of tiny creatures inside my undershirt, causing me to itch and scratch until I could no longer stand it and yelled for Mom. On with the blinding lights. Off with my nightwear and undershirt while Mom searched every inch of my clothes and body until she found the black culprits the size of a speck of dust. When she caught one, she said, "Make sure you pinch it well. These fleas are not dead until you see the red color of their blood or they will come back to bite you." Then she quickly searched and snatched another one. The fleas always seem to pick the middle of the night, leaving me their trademark of pus, scabs and scars. If it wasn't fleas or cockroaches, it was mosquitoes or flies swarming and buzzing around my head. No matter how many times I pulled my blanket over my head or tried to swat them away, they circled back to sing in my ears.

Back to the story when Joanne and I ventured into the hallway while Mom left the building for more fabric: Muriel, my "goody-good" sister, shook her head and stubbornly repeated, "Mommie told us not to," and she closed the door after us. We heard rumors that someone saw a Boogie Man in the hall, and I wanted to catch a glimpse of him, so we went chasing after our friends who had disappeared in different directions. Minutes later, not having any luck, Joanne and I knew we had better get back before Mom came home or worse yet… before the Boogie Man spotted us.

We tried to open the door to our apartment, but the door was chained. We did not know Mom came home, found that Joanne and I had defied her orders, and forbade Muriel to open the door. Joanne and I pounded with our fists until they hurt.

"Please, let us in," we pleaded and wailed. "We promise not to do this again."

Every neighbor in the building heard us, but no one came to our rescue. After what seemed like hours, we were exhausted, our voices hoarse. Finally we heard Muriel climb a stool to unlatch the chain. We entered and begged for Mom's forgiveness. Maybe if Marilyn was home, we would all be safe from Mom's ire, because Marilyn would not have allowed us out into the hall and we probably would have listened to her.

Some of the best times we had living in San Francisco were when Mom let us go up on the tar-and-gravel roof of our apartment building to play while she took down the wash, which she had hung up in the morning as early as five o'clock. While she chatted with the other tenants, Joanne and I would sneak around behind the sheets and the laundry hanging on the lines and play "hide and seek," hiding from Mom or other tenant children. Certain areas of the roof were designated off-limits with chicken wire to keep us away from loose gravel and the edges of the roof, but somehow we would manage to pull and claw at the chicken wire, crawl and squeeze through a small opening, and hide in the "forbidden" areas. Standing close to the edge of the roof, nearly four stories up, and peeking over the sides with my outstretched neck, I could see below the yard of the YMCA where I attended nursery school. It was a long way down, even with the use of the metal fire escapes. Seeing this and not liking heights made me shudder.

While she was away in Belmont, Marilyn missed a very special day, special because we were attending Joanne's kindergarten graduation ceremony at St. Mary's, and special because it was a full day's outing at the park, with Dad dressed in his suit and tie. We were also dressed up in our Sunday best: Joanne in a new white organdy party dress that cost Mom ten dollars and a fluffy white bow Mom bought at I. Magnin for forty cents. The bow was stunning atop Joanne's short, thick Shirley Temple curls that framed her face and accentuated her big brown eyes. Mom wore high heels and carried a matching leather purse. Muriel, wearing a white blouse, a short skirt, and a pair of white shoes, could not stop fidgeting and flipping her skirt at the hem. I wore a white button-down-front print dress with a Peter Pan collar and a pair of black Mary Jane shoes. Dad, our hair-cutter that morning, had just neatly trimmed Muriel's and my straight hair and bangs. Mom, proud of how she had combed our hair, asked a friend to take our pictures.

During the year-and-a-half that Marilyn was away, she learned to speak English and ate American meals. The rest of us spoke very little English and ate rice three meals a day. When Marilyn returned home at age eight, she relearned to speak Chinese, and once again her role was to keep an eye on us.

Later, Mom was told Marilyn did not have tuberculosis after all, but was quarantined as a preventive measure. Waiting for Marilyn when she arrived home was a fancy white bow just like Joanne's. For years to come, the responsibility that came with being the first-born never left Marilyn. I know, and I would rather not trade places with her. I like being the middle child. I like being the third-born. Three is my favorite number—my lucky number. I like where I am.

CHAPTER FIVE:

A SWINGING TIME

In 1944, while World War II was still going on, I attended kindergarten at the Commodore Stockton Elementary School at Jackson and Powell Streets. I remember a boy in my class with my name, but his was spelled with an "i," as in Francis. I remember trudging up the steep hill to school each morning; it seemed like a mile walk. During recess, I would stand out on the schoolyard and look across at the older students playing in the upper yard. I wished I was one of them, having fun chasing and laughing.

After school in first grade, I attended Chinese classes with Joanne at the Baptist Church on Waverly Place, across the street from our apartment building. Mom wanted us to learn to read and write Chinese, and she stressed the importance of getting an education. Our teacher, round-faced, balding and wearing thick horn-rimmed glasses, was strict and carried a foot-long wooden ruler, which he did not hesitate to use to whack a student who stepped out of line or gave a wrong answer. He ruled by fear and we feared the ruler.

Next to the church on an upslope was the Chinatown Playground, which was surrounded on three sides by a tall chain-link fence. An entrance gate on Waverly Place led directly into the basketball courts. Up a few concrete steps was the main level with slides, monkey bars and a row of swings for older children. Near the clubhouse, which was torn down in 1977 and rebuilt in 1980, was a play area with more swings for babies and toddlers. Up a long flight of steps were the tennis and volleyball courts. From there, a gate opened to Pagoda Alley, where the famous Hang Ah Teahouse served on the second floor a variety of Chinese dim sum delicacies and pastries.

Every day at Chinese School I would wait anxiously for recess. One time I bolted out of class at the sound of the bell, dashed across the basketball courts, darted up the steps, and claimed my swing. I took a few steps forward and then a few steps back to put the swing in motion. The cool wind on my cheeks felt great as strands of my short hair blew wildly in front of my eyes. I never wanted to stop, as I used my legs to help propel the swing higher and higher like a pendulum… further and further, because I wanted to touch the sky like a bird.

What seemed like only minutes later, our teacher leaned out of one of the windows facing the park and rang a big bell like a madman to warn us we had just minutes to get back into his classroom or receive a hard knock or two on top of our heads with his knuckle or the ruler. All the classmates made a bee-line straight out of the park and I wanted to be right behind them so that I would not be late, at least not walk in by myself.

I tried to drag my leaded feet along the ground to stop swinging, but my legs barely touched the ground. The swing swayed from side to side and spun out of control. Both my hands turned red from the grip I had on the chains, which clanged against each other. I loosened my grip and jumped, tumbling onto the ground, dirtying my dress, scraping my hands and knees and scuffing my brown high-top leather shoes. I could just hear Mom lecturing me to be good and listen to the teacher. I knew I had to hurry back into the classroom now… or else face the ruler!

I raced to exit Sacramento Street, but now that gate was locked and apparently the park director had left for the day. Like a spider I clawed my way up the cyclone fence, pushing one foot after the other through the open mesh. The top of the fence had spikes with sharp metal points to keep people like me off. I felt I was eight feet off the ground as I carefully lifted each leg over the top to avoid getting cut. One of the spikes caught the skirt of my dress, slowing me as I jumped. I tumbled onto the rough sidewalk and further scraped my knees. I quickly brushed the dirt and loose gravel off my dress and knees as I hobbled up a flight of stairs, getting in line just as a couple of latecomers pushed and scurried behind me. The teacher, a scowl on his face, was there to greet me with his wooden ruler. He took a swing at me, I ducked, and the stick hit the student behind me, which made him, as well as our teacher, very MAD at me. I had yet to face Mom when she would see my soiled dress, scraped knees and scuffed-up shoes.

All I learned to write in Chinese that year were the numbers from one to ten and my last name, FONG.

Our Chinese lessons ended when Mom made a decision to move away. All along, Mom heard horror stories about young girls in Chinatown running around with dirty old men, many of whom left their wives in China. Mom also did not approve of girls who elope or marry out of their race. Some girls ran away after being promised wonderful jobs, only to be lured and confined into prostitution, or treated as commodities. Others ended up hiding at the Presbyterian-sponsored Donaldina Cameron House on Sacramento Street to escape mistreatment, if they were lucky enough to escape. Mom also observed girls holding low-paying jobs like restaurant cashiers and sales clerks; to her, their futures looked unpromising. She wanted a better life for her daughters and did not want us to fall into these same traps.

Mom decided to move us out of San Francisco to a safe and better place… and maybe to a neighborhood with swings.

CHAPTER SIX:
WEST OAKLAND

In 1946, when Mrs. Fong Cho Git, a relative we addressed as *Bok Moo,* heard Mom was looking to move, she told Mom about a piece of real estate for sale across the bay from San Francisco in West Oakland, catty-corner from *Bok Moo's* "mom and pop" grocery store which was named Sixteenth Street Market. Uncle Donald, Dad's younger brother, accompanied Mom to see the property at 1112 – 16th Street, between Adeline and Chestnut streets. The neighborhood, made up mostly of white people and small two-story homes on square blocks of flatland, seemed nice and quiet—unlike the congestion and the crowdedness of the tall buildings in hilly San Francisco. Living in Oakland was warmer than foggy San Francisco, a Key System streetcar ran in front of our house, and the "A" train, which was the main means of mass transportation from our neighborhood to San Francisco, was just a few blocks away. What Mom liked about this piece of real estate was it generated income that could help her pay our monthly mortgage.

A block away on Adeline was DeFremery Park with lots of swings. Oh boy, oh boy!

Our two-story, four-unit, brown shingle apartment building had a large front yard elevated about two feet above the sidewalk with a cement wall. One set of concrete steps and a smaller set of wooden stairs led to the small wooden front porch. The front door, with rows of small windowpanes and black paint peeling from the blazing hot sun, led into a central hallway with a fancy banister that my sisters and I could slide down when Mom wasn't home to catch us. Carpeted stairs marked the way to the two upstairs units. The previous owner, Mrs. Campbell, sold the building furnished, which included two non-matching Mission Style oak rocking chairs in the upstairs hall.

Uncle Donald earned a good living during the war years by working at the shipyards and amassed quite a sum of money. He wanted to make a generous gift of $2,000 to Marilyn toward the house, but Mom accepted the money only on the condition it was a loan that Mom was to repay. With this $2,000 loan, plus $2,000 she redeemed from buying savings bonds while working at Simmons, and a $2,000 mortgage loan from the San Francisco Chinatown branch of the Bank of America, Mom purchased the house and was very proud that she paid, as she put it, "all cash" to the seller.

We moved into the smaller unit on the lower floor. It had a living room with cream-colored wood paneling halfway up the walls; in one corner was a built-in, triangular-shaped wood cabinet with shelves and glass doors. Shades on rollers and lace curtains covered the tall windows. The single bedroom housed the double bed moved from San Francisco that was a wedding gift from Mom's "brothers," and a brown portable closet made of flimsy cardboard laminated to look like wood. The two narrow doors that clung onto the metal hinges could barely stay latched. Mom placed her sewing machine in front of the wall with the tall window.

My sisters and I slept in the living room on two sofas and a new day bed, like a trundle bed that opened at night to sleep two. I no longer had the army cot that was my bed in San Francisco, which I used to assemble each night by pushing two long wooden poles through the casings of the heavy canvas, and take apart each morning. When I lay down in the cot, it sagged like a flimsy hammock, giving no support, but at least it was better than the rattan chair I had slept on before I got the cot.

Beyond the bedroom was a small kitchen with an old Wedgewood stove that had all burners working, a white sink, and a boxy, cream-colored, four-door wooden ice box. For twenty-five cents, we bought a block of ice and placed it inside one of the metal-lined compartments. When the ice melted and dripped into a pan placed under the ice box, all we had to do was discard the water so it would not overflow onto the floor. It was a small price to pay to keep our food cold and fresh.

Next to the kitchen was a small bathroom with a wash basin, a toilet and a cast-iron bathtub that sat on four legs. Gone were the trips down the hall to empty our waste! When we pulled a long metal chain attached to a square water tank above the toilet, water flushed away all the contents in the toilet. Gone were the trips to the roof to hang the wash! Now we had our own clotheslines in the backyard. Gone was the washtub in the kitchen where Mom bathed us and climbed in to take her baths! Now we had a real bathtub and the two concrete washtubs on the back porch were for washing clothes. Mom said, "Of all the things in our apartment, I love the bathtub, wash basin and toilet because these were the things I wanted for my girls." I know now how she loved us.

Mrs. Campbell, now our tenant, lived upstairs in the unit above us. Across the hall from her were two more tenants, Mrs. Walsh and her son Francis Foley. A driver for the Carnation Milk Company, Francis wore a uniform as white as the bottles of milk he delivered to his customers' doorsteps. Shortly after we moved in, Mrs. Campbell died in an automobile accident, and much to Mom's surprise, she received twenty dollars as part of the inheritance from Mrs. Campbell's estate. Mom must have been on her good list. For the next seven years, tenants came and went. One tenant downstairs tried to teach my sisters and me to read and write Chinese. Another tenant, when she heard I had a cold, took Muriel and me to DeFremery Park because "the fresh air would do me good." Later, the Snyders from Oklahoma moved in across the hall from us with their teenage daughter and a young son. Country music played all day long in their apartment. The lyrics were sad, but nevertheless the music grew on me, like my favorite, "Tennessee Waltz" sung by Patti Page. Mom did not mind us spending time at the Snyders because they were down-to-earth; their hospitality was warm, and Mom trusted them.

Like the Low family in San Francisco, the Fong Cho Git family had a lot of children to keep us company: Stanley, who was Marilyn's age; Arthur, whose age was between Joanne and me; Myron, who was in Muriel's class; and there were three older sisters, Eva, Rose and Ruby. They lived upstairs above their store; the children helped out by cashiering, stocking the shelves and sweeping the floors. *Bok Moo* often invited us for turkey dinner at Christmas time. Although there was an outside entrance to their unit upstairs, we would take a shortcut through the store into the dingy storeroom in the back and to a second set of stairs, like a secret passage, up to their living quarters. I stared in wonder at the stock of canned goods on the shelves—many covered with dust and discolored labels: Van Camp Pork and Beans, maple syrup that came in tin cans the shape of a log cabin, Spam ham and Quaker Oatmeal, in the tall round cardboard containers.

Next to their store was a butcher shop owned by the children's uncle and next to that a Chinese laundry. As Stanley Fong got older, he learned to perform magic tricks, and often entertained us when we all went over for a visit. Mom felt bad she could never reciprocate by inviting them over for dinner.

Mom continued to sew, with bundles of fabric delivered from San Francisco to our home, racing to meet the deadline for the weekly pick-up of her finished garments—soft pastel rayon crepe blouses, trimmed at the neck and sleeves with cording. Whenever I got into a dispute with one of my sisters or tried to tattle-tale, Mom would not permit us to argue. Instead, she'd say to me, "Never mind; pull up a chair and sit by me. Keep me company." I felt protected and special, like the times Dad let me sit with him when we lived in San Francisco. Mom was a fast seamstress and she made her sewing machine roar. Soliciting our help, Mom taught us to turn the long narrow cording for the blouses using a skinny rod with a hook on the end that Mom made out of a metal coat hanger. The tedious work made my fingers sore, but I enjoyed helping and watching Mom sew. I also felt useful.

Mom timed her monthly trips to San Francisco on the "A" train to make the mortgage payments on her 30-year loan. She collected $30 rent from each of the three units and applied all $90 to her regular $30 payment, thus quadrupling each payment to $120. Realizing in a year's time that the loan was paid down to $500 and shuddering at the thought she would be in her mid-60s before the loan would be fully paid off, she took in more sewing at night and weekends to pay off the balance as well as other outstanding loans. Mom did not like owing anyone; but I never knew how savvy Mom was with money. She figured it out on her own and she was brilliant as a money manager. I hope she passed that ability on to me.

With our move to Oakland in 1946, I entered second grade at Lafayette Elementary School, located at West and Eighteenth streets. My classmates teased me for not speaking English and for my accent. After a while, I hid the fact I knew Chinese, but the teasing did not stop because my accent would not go away. My High 2nd/Low 3rd combined class in 1947 had one Spanish girl (Gladys) several African Americans (Judith, Mona, Velma and June), and several Caucasians (Louise, Beatrice, Glenda and Wanda). Diane and Gayle were the two with the pretty curls and ringlets. Others in class were Ronnie and my next door neighbor, Jerry, who lived on the corner of Chestnut Street. There were two Japanese students (Yoshio and Margie) and I was the only Chinese girl in my class of thirty students.

I remember the time a big dog followed my three sisters and me to school. We were taking our usual route, walking east on Sixteenth Street—what seemed like miles—and had just passed the D. J. Canty Hardware Store, an old one-story wooden building with a faded sign that said "HARDWARE, PAINTS and GLASS"; this was the only retail store on the block in the residential area of West Oakland. The faster I walked, the closer the dog came running behind me. I did not want the dog to lick or bite me, so I ran, zigzagging back and forth across the street. Not daring to look back, I could hear the dog panting and its footsteps gaining on me as I turned left on Market Street. Nearly out of breath and panting louder than the dog, I was relieved to see an adult traffic monitor in a red windbreaker at the corner of Eighteenth Street. She held up her red octagon "STOP" sign with one hand and halted traffic with the other. Seeing the exasperation and fear on my face, she assured me in her booming, jovial voice, "Oh honey, this dog will not hurt you. He just wants you to play." I crossed the street and made my way into the schoolyard, where it was safe for me to see if my sisters had made it too. Yes, they were okay.

To this day, I am still afraid to visit friends who have dogs and cats unless these pets are placed in rooms behind closed doors.

We walked home for lunch every day where Mom would prepare something simple, like rice with steamed eggs or salted fish. When times got tough, we mixed our bowls of rice with a spoonful of lard and drops of soy sauce for flavor. I loved my small white one-cup-capacity enamel bowl with the blue rim, stamped on the bottom "made in Kockums, Sweden," and my pair of short red plastic chopsticks. We trudged home for lunch in scorching hot heat. We trudged home in the pouring rain. The worst was when we were caught in a downpour without rain gear or umbrellas. On those days, my hair got sopping wet and rainwater seeped through the holes in the bottom of my shoes, drenching my socks. Back and forth, four terribly long trips a day. Muriel, however, remembers fried egg sandwiches and Dad walking us back to school on rainy days under his large black umbrella.

and ran up and down the wide staircase in the center of the hall to their rooms. After a short program, the members served us refreshments and sent each of us home with gifts. I am not sure whether we were chosen because we were smart or because we were poor or both. However, I enjoyed being treated.

This reminded me of the times in San Francisco when we often stood outside our apartment building to watch members of the Salvation Army, wearing navy hats and uniforms trimmed in red, gather to preach the gospel of God and to sing praises to the Lord across the street on Waverly Place. Some of the members were part of a small band blaring out tunes on their instruments. At Christmas, the staff would welcome a long line of children for a holiday party and send each of us home with a huge gift stocking made of stiff, rough, orange mesh, bulging at the seams with small toys, crayons, a coloring book, candy canes and oranges. Santa did not come to our apartment, so this was the only way we received gifts. That put a smile on my face.

In Oakland, as I grew older, I wanted to know if there really was a Santa. One Christmas Eve, I secretly stayed up all night and peeked out the sides of the long roller shade on one of the living room windows, hoping to catch a glimpse of Santa and his reindeer as they passed in front of the moon, like I had seen in pictures. He did not appear, leaving me disappointed, but in the morning, much to my surprise and like magic, my sisters and I found a small stocking for each of us, filled with a couple of dimes. There was a Santa after all!

Throughout the year, if Mom happened to realize it was one of our birthdays, she would send the birthday celebrant to the corner store with a quarter for a box of cornflakes while one of us ran gleefully into the bathroom for four sheets of toilet paper, into which Mom used to pour out equal amounts of cereal because she did not want us to fight over who had more or less. One time I picked Cheerios as my treat and another time it was shredded wheat (the Nabisco plant was a few blocks away on Fourteenth Street). After trying shredded wheat in a bowl of milk, I decided I did not like it because I could not finish eating the whole bowl before the cereal shredded apart and became soggy. Sometimes we used the palms of our hands as cups to hold our treats because Mom did not know about buying paper napkins or paper towels.

Mom did not play favorites; she gave us equal shares, whether it was a piece of cake, a slice of orange, or a few dried beetles which she purchased from a street vendor in San Francisco Chinatown. She poured the delicacy, which came in a small brown paper bag, into the palms of our outstretched hands and taught us how to remove the inedible wings before eating the rest of the insect. It was like performing surgery.

If I complained that one sister got more, or her share was bigger, Mom would stammer, "Go weigh it."

I would have, except we did not have a scale and I knew better than to sass or challenge Mom, even though I knew she was wrong.

CHAPTER SEVEN:

LEMON DROPS

At times I was so hungry, I often stole a penny or two from the drawer where Mom kept a few coins. After school I would go straight to the little store across from Lafayette School and buy Kits (small one-inch-square chewy candy in chocolate, strawberry or banana flavors, individually wrapped in waxed paper), Tootsie Rolls, Bit-O-Honey (chewy honey-flavored taffy candy with bits of almonds in a red-and-yellow wrapper) or Neccos (a tube of round chocolate wafer candy). I would gobble them down—the only time I ate fast—before anyone, especially Mom, saw me; otherwise, it meant punishment.

In one corner of our living room sat a china cabinet with glass doors where Mom kept a small jar of lemon drops on one of the lower shelves. When visitors dropped by, it was important that we had something to serve besides tea, like a slice of cake, a dish of cookies, or at least some candy. It was equally important that when we went to visit someone, we never went empty-handed. My mouth watered just thinking about those yellow oval-shaped candies. The taste reminded me of times I had eaten whole fresh lemons, puckering my mouth like a prune and etching my teeth like sandpaper as I sucked on the pulp and juice. The gradual erosion of the thin layers of enamel on my teeth, along with multiple cavities, proved to be costly, which I will describe in a later chapter.

Yes, as a child, I was hungry all the time. All day long I heard rubber bands of hunger snap inside my stomach. When there was food to eat, I would mull over each bite because every bite was precious to me, and I wanted the taste and flavors to linger forever in my mouth. Many times after dinner I was still hungry, but I dared not ask for more when I could see that no more food was on the table.

One time I went up to Mom's china cabinet, opened the glass doors, unscrewed the candy jar lid, and took out one lemon drop. Days later, when Mom discovered the empty jar, she called my sisters and me together and lined us up in a row. "Okay, who did it?" she asked, but I was not going to take all the blame for the empty jar. None of us admitted it, so Mom decided to punish all four of us, saying it was also for all the times we did naughty things but did not get caught. I think Mom's attempt to be fair was unfair! This time she did not use a chopstick to spank our hands and legs. According to Mom, we were too old to spank. Instead, she told us to kneel at the foot of her double bed while she resumed sewing. Later she crawled into bed, although it was the middle of the afternoon, and yet did not tell us we could get up and leave the room. It seemed the sun went down and the moon came up. Mom still did not say a word.

My sisters and I shivered on the cold linoleum floor, afraid to speak or move. I slowly traced the circular patterns of flowers on the red linoleum floor, picking up dirt and dust with my index finger and pretending to play jacks on the same floor. I dreamed of happier times when we got our first set of jacks and a tiny red rubber ball. We would laugh as we tried to master the game and be the winner, like the times we played hopscotch, jumped rope or learned to adjust our new metal roller skates with skate keys and skate on the rough concrete sidewalk in front of our house.

In the meantime, kneeling on the floor, the lack of blood circulation made my legs go numb and I could no longer stay up on my knees. All I could do was shift my weight from side to side and squeeze my cheeks to keep from making a puddle on the floor because I was afraid to sneak away to the bathroom. My sisters and I glanced back and forth at each other. The minutes and the hours ticked away, and we knew it was approaching dinner time. My stomach growled; then my stomach spoke to me again. Since my sisters and I rotated daily duties, it was my turn tonight to make dinner. I knew if dinner was not ready when Mom woke up from her nap, she would be very angry at all of us, yet if I made a single sound advancing toward the kitchen, she would accuse me of purposely waking her and depriving her of sleep. What a dilemma! No matter what I did, it was always wrong. In silence, I questioned why I was being punished in this manner. Eventually Mom woke up and we were allowed to leave the room.

At other times when we begged forgiveness, Mom granted it if she was in the right mood. If not, Mom carried on for days, weeks, months, even years it seems, not telling us what she was mad about. We did not know when she would speak to us, so that everything would be normal again. Silence is not golden, as I sensed and dreaded that kind of tension in the air.

One time when Mom was angry and not speaking to us, our doorbell rang. Mom was very sociable and often invited people over to visit, so she let one of us answer the door. She received the guests in a friendly manner, acting as if nothing was wrong. As the guests were leaving, she said her usual gracious departing words in our Shekki or Loong Du dialect, "When you have time, come visit again." Then she turned to us, broke her silence, and continued to talk to us like everything was okay. That time we were literally saved by the bell.

CHAPTER EIGHT:

HEALTH, WELFARE AND AN ORANGE COAT

As I stated in the last chapter, eating fresh lemons as fruit eroded the thin layers of enamel on my teeth. As a child, I did not have good dental care. I did not even have floss or a toothbrush. Mom sent me to the dentist only after I repeatedly complained of an excruciating toothache. I remember my early visits to a county clinic with a long row of dental chairs facing a white wall. I remember squirming on the smooth, cold leather seat as a dentist wearing a white uniform pumped his foot on a pedal, lifting my chair well off the floor and leaving my legs dangling. Water from a narrow plastic tube swirled around a shallow porcelain bowl next to my chair. I stared at the ripples, mesmerized by the circular patterns. Patients around me gagged as they spit and gargled into their bowls.

I leaned back against the two "door knobs" holding the back of my head. The light blinded me, except when the dentist's head loomed large in front of it, giving my eyes a respite. When I saw him staring, I rolled my eyes to dodge his direct gaze. I wanted to chuckle when his eyebrows fluttered just inches from my face. I tried not to watch him inject the anesthesia Novocain, because feeling the needle puncturing my gums was more painful than the dental work itself. From the blink of my eyes, a single tear drop found its way down my cheek. The drill hissed like an electric saw. I held my breath. He filled one cavity, then another.

When we moved to Oakland, I went to Dr. Lester Lee, one of the dentists in Chinatown. With Mom's higher-paying job in the early 1950s sewing at Little Lady's Lingerie on Twelfth Street, she was able to pay for some of our dental work, but still I did not go until I had a bad toothache. Dr. Lee filled one cavity, then another, and another. Ouch!!

Gone today is the smell of amalgam. Gone are the porcelain spit bowls. Gone are the old drills, replaced by high-speed drills that cause no pain and make no noise. X-rays in color immediately pop up on large computer screens. Patients can change television channels by using remote controls. I prefer easy listening music to lull me into dreamland, and I don't flinch an inch or utter a sound. Because of losing four upper front teeth in 1955, I now have implants, and I do not mind going to the dentist or sitting in a dental chair for hours while being worked on.

On hot, sweltering days when we were living in San Francisco, Mom would set our white wooden child's table with two chairs in the hallway outside our apartment and let us play where it was cooler. Those were the times Mom treated us to dishes of refreshing tofu, soft soy bean cakes she bought right out of the large open tin cans from a store down the street. Those were also the times my body got sticky and sweaty and my nose bled often because of the heat. One day I looked down and saw bright-red drops of blood on my clean white cotton undershirt; I yelled for Mom, who stopped her sewing and came running.

"Keep your chin up and your head back on the chair," she said. She pressed her thumb and index finger on the front of my throat, feeling for my pulse. "Push firmly against these two same spots while I go get a wet towel," she said and quickly disappeared into the apartment. I tried to duplicate the same pressure with my fingers. I gulped several times to keep from gagging on the globs of blood gushing down my throat—a strange, bitter taste. The damp facecloth Mom neatly folded and placed on my forehead kept slipping. She turned it over to the cool side, which warmed quickly from my hot forehead. The bleeding did not stop. Mom left hastily again and returned with a long stalk of green onions. "Here, stick the root-end up your nostril. If the bleeding does not stop soon, I will call the doctor." It seemed forever, but luckily it did stop. It must have been the smell of the onion.

In Oakland, I continued to get nosebleeds, as the weather was even warmer there than in San Francisco. One time my nose bled so profusely, Mom took me on the bus to see Dr. Jacob Yee, a family physician in Chinatown. Taking out a long strand of thick, white cotton puff (the kind the beauticians use around the hairlines of their customers to keep the permanent chemicals from dripping down their faces and necks), he soaked it in a solution and using long tweezers, he stuffed it up my nose. I could feel as it went up and down my long nasal passage until it nearly touched my throat and I almost fainted from the fumes. I wanted to sneeze but did not want to splatter blood on Dr. Yee. He put gauze and white tape across my bulging nostrils, leaving bits of cotton exposed. He said if the bleeding did not stop, he would have to cauterize my nose. I shuddered at the thought, even though I did not know what the word meant, but it sounded painful. We would know about the bleeding in a couple of days at my next appointment.

On the way home, all eyes on the bus were staring at me. I felt like Rudolph, the Red-Nosed Reindeer, except my nose was all bandaged white, with bits of cotton poking through the gauze and tapes. At my follow-up appointment, Dr. Yee removed the tape. He slowly removed the blood-soaked strand of cotton out of my nose. In places where the cotton stuck, it tickled as he wiggled and tugged on it. Ouch! Fortunately, the bleeding had stopped. This time going home, I did not notice anyone on the bus staring at me, but my nose was still very red and swollen.

In school, I usually sat in the first two rows of the

classroom—alphabetically assigned or by my choice, because I wanted to see and be attentive. Tall or rowdy students, and kids who wanted to goof off or hide from the teacher, always seemed to sit toward the back of the room. In elementary school, my eyesight progressively worsened, to the point where things written on the blackboard were very difficult to read. I made good guesses at the written words, but when it came to numbers, preciseness was difficult. I winked one eye, then the other, cocked my head, and opened both eyes wide, but eventually all the tricks I tried no longer worked. I could not distinguish zero from six, one from seven, four from nine, nor three from eight.

I was afraid to tell Mom I needed glasses. We never asked for anything or complained, until things got unbearable, like a really bad toothache. Then in the sixth grade, when even sitting in the front row no longer helped, I raised my hand and asked for permission to walk up to the blackboard. I felt my nose touch the board and rub off chalk as I tried to make out the numbers. I continued to do poorly on my test scores and my grades continued to go down. My teacher must have noticed the drop in my test scores and suspected I needed glasses because shortly after that, the school nurse called me into her office, gave me a brief eye test and sent a note home to Mom requesting I have a full eye examination. Marilyn took me on the bus to the Alameda County Highland Hospital on Fourteenth Avenue and MacArthur Boulevard. The enormous stony-gray building sat high on a slope, surrounded by homes and apartment buildings. We made our way to the main entrance, climbing the shallow concrete steps. The examiner dilated my eyes with eye-drops, and then administered the test. We left the building and walked straight out into blinding light. I slipped my right hand under Marilyn's left arm, clasping it tightly without saying a word as she guided me slowly back down the flight of steps to the bus stop. Everything in sight was orange, and I could not keep my eyes open or see where I was going because of the powerful glare. I thought I was going blind, but I was glad

Marilyn was with me all the way. I dreaded the idea I may be going blind.

A few weeks later, I had a pair of glasses, nice and thick… and ugly. They kept slipping down my nose, but once I adjusted to them, I saw and read things I had not noticed before, like billboards and street names, and my test scores improved. Later on, regarding my glasses, Mom said to me, "If you had only told me, I would have bought them for you sooner."

Four eyes are better than two. Who can argue with that… except the teasers?

As we were growing up, Mom taught us manners by emphasizing at the dinner table, "Don't be greedy. Don't take more than your share, and try not to reach across to the other side of the table with your chopsticks for a bigger or better piece of meat." I surmise that meant to look at the food on the table, see the number of people eating and determine the fair share each one gets. Then I noticed she would take the neck or the rear end of the chicken for herself. From the shallow dish of steamed fish, she gave us the pieces of meat while she would suck on the bones and eyeballs. Eventually, I too learned to eat fish carefully and feel for the tiny bones in my mouth so that I would not swallow and choke on them. I learned for myself that meat around the bone usually had the best flavor, like when Mom fried pork chops or stewed fish heads with garlic and chunks of fresh tomatoes.

As I got older, I thought our family would qualify for welfare and for years I thought Mom was too proud to apply for assistance. The truth was, Mom told me, she never applied for welfare because she feared we could all be deported if the government found out she and my dad had come to America illegally.

One time when Mom heard that an agency downtown was passing out food, she sent my sisters and me to stand in line for the giveaways of powdered milk and powdered eggs. We tried to use the products, but stopped when Mom decided these did not fit into our daily diet of Chinese food and rice.

In grammar school, I was the class monitor chosen by my teacher to help pass out trays of milk and cookies during recess. Once, when I saw my name listed twice, I tried to explain to my teacher that Mom had paid for just one order, but my teacher assured me it was okay. Maybe she knew something I didn't, but every morning at school I drank two cartons of milk and had double servings of graham crackers. After that, I was never hungry in the mornings. Being a slow eater, the problem I had was getting all the milk and crackers down in a short time.

Muriel and I wore hand-me-down clothes from Marilyn and Joanne, who sometimes got their hand-me-downs from second cousin Bess. One day Mom turned to Muriel and me and said, "Let's go shopping," and she took the two of us downtown. I think I was in the fifth grade. We walked past the old Payless Drug Store on Telegraph and Eighteenth where my sisters and I sat many times in the big chairs on the mezzanine floor to have our hair permed with rollers attached by spiral coils to electricity. That was the only way my hair turned out with Shirley Temple curls like Joanne had in kindergarten. We continued walking several more blocks to Twenty-Seventh Street and entered Sears Department Store. "Go ahead, pick out any coat you want," said Mom as we stopped at the children's coat department on the first floor. "It is time you each get your own new coat." I had fun spinning one rack after another, as I watched the different styles and colors whiz past my outstretched fingers. It was as if my hand was playing piano on the hangers. One coat caught my eye—an orange one. It was wool, with large lapels and an A-line shaped skirt that flared out from the princess waist. It fit me perfectly. I twirled around in it as if it was already mine. Mom kept her promise as she pulled out her money to pay, happy that she could afford to buy us new coats for the winter. For me, it was like getting a gift at Christmas, which was rare.

Another time my sisters and I received free vouchers to pick out clothes at Franklin Elementary School in East

Oakland. Marilyn took us on a #40 bus to East Fifteenth and Ninth Avenue. The huge room in an old building was dim except for the sunlight beaming through the windows. Large tables were piled high with donated clothing and shoes. Some things were brand-new, and others were used but in good, clean shape. The workers greeted us warmly. They led us from section to section, picking out a set number of dresses, underwear, socks, sweaters and other items. In the shoe section, I tried on several pairs, but they were too wide or too long for my feet. I found a pair of black suede shoes with low wedge heels and three straps across the front that buckled to one side. When I turned the shoes over to look at the bottom, I saw no holes… I grinned, knowing these will not let water soak through to my socks on rainy days! They could be my dress shoes, and they fit. I continued checking items off my list, creating a pile on the counter of things just for me.

All the way home on the bus, I clutched the bags with my new wardrobe. We could hardly wait to show Mom what we shopped for, and the bargains did not cost us a penny! They were gifts. It was better than spending Christmas at the Salvation Army in San Francisco. This time I had gotten a pair of shoes, and they would do just fine when I started junior high school in the fall.

CHAPTER NINE:

VICKIE MAKES FIVE

I was a sickly, anemic child. Every time I took a blood test, like at the County Public Health Department, I would feel faint and shake afterwards. One time, Mom ran to the water fountain and brought back a paper cup filled with water. "Here, drink this and you'll feel better," she said as I gulped it down. The cold water calmed me. Between my ailments and my bloody noses, Mom was constantly sending me to see doctors. Another time when I was fighting to breathe and having an asthma attack, Mom gave me a big pill, but my body reacted to it and my condition worsened. That was when I started sleeping with Mom in her double bed in Oakland, as she was a source of comfort to me.

I slept at the foot of the bed across the width of the mattress. When she got into bed her icy-cold feet touched my nose, prompting me to turn my head away to keep from smelling her feet. The bed was cold, like the linoleum floor. I trembled and shivered under the covers, but felt better curling into a ball next to Mom's body. Sometimes she would shriek when my hands or body accidentally touched her. Eventually our bodies warmed up from the layers of blankets she piled up on the bed.

The handmade comforter Mom brought along with our household items from San Francisco was especially heavy. She had sewn odd-sized large squares of red and other colors of printed cotton remnants into two large sheets, like patchwork, then sewed the two sheets together and layered thick batting between them. Since Mom did not tuft it in places like a real quilt, over time the batting shifted and the blanket became lumpy. One night when I became hot and sweaty, I tried to kick off the layers of bedding, but they were heavy and there were too many. I tried to turn one corner of the quilt away from my mouth so I could breathe, but it flapped back in place. Mom would surely get mad if I awakened her to help me. Exhausted as if I had just fought a boxing match, I finally fell asleep.

For months, I noticed Mom's stomach getting large. When I made a remark about her condition, she placed her arms across her chest, shrugged her shoulders and swayed from side to side, childlike. "It is only gas. I am sitting too long and sewing too much. It will go away," she said with a little grin. Months went by and each day she moved slower than the day before. I wondered why she did not stop sewing. When she announced she was going to have a baby, I asked, "How do you get a baby?" "Oh, the doctor brings the baby in a satchel," she replied and I did not question her any further.

A few weeks later, Mom yelled, "It's time! Quick, dial Kellogg 3-0811 for Dr. Lamb and watch for her to arrive." Except for Marilyn, who was born in a hospital in San Francisco Chinatown, Joanne, Muriel and I were delivered at home in our San Francisco apartment by Dr. S. Lamb, a Caucasian lady married to a Chinese doctor. Now this time, their daughter, Dr. Loris Lamb, who had an office on Haley Avenue in Oakland, was coming to help Mom with the delivery. Kneeling on the sofa in the living room and watching from the front window, I saw Dr. Lamb arrive with two black leather bags. She came up the steps, headed straight into the bedroom and closed the door. Two bags surely meant Mom was going to have twins; I was hopeful that at least one baby would be a boy. Then Mom might stop saying when she was angry with us, "If I had just one son, I would not have any of you." *Mom does not remember ever saying this to us.*

There was a lot of commotion in the other room as my sisters and I sat quietly in the living room. Hours later, a healthy baby cry bellowed from the bedroom. Mom had just given birth to her fifth child—another girl, so tiny and fragile. I was the smallest at birth, at six pounds eight ounces, my other three sisters each averaged around seven pounds and this one was Mom's heaviest baby, at just a little over eight pounds. That was July 21, 1948, Mom was thirty-eight years old and I was nine. As she did when she chose each of our first names, Mom listened to Dr. Lamb read from a list of girls' names. Mom did not want an ordinary name like Mary or Anna. No names of flowers like Rose or Lily. No gemstones like Pearl or Ruby. She had already picked "Mehlan, Jo Yan, Fansersee and Mehleeyo," the best she could pronounce our American names in English. This time Mom stopped at "Victolia" and named her newborn daughter Victoria after the San Francisco neighbor's son, Victor, because "victory" meant "winner." Mom also gave Vickie, as we called her for short, the Chinese name *York Bun*, meaning Dignified and Well-Mannered. Mom believed in giving good Chinese names with strong meanings. Dr. Lamb congratulated Mom and left an invoice, which Mom paid-in-full seven days later. Vickie's delivery cost Mom $150 and a certified birth certificate was one dollar.

Then for days following, when friends and relatives came to visit, Mom served them bowls of soup cooked with chicken, mushrooms, ginger and whiskey, and pigs' feet cooked tender with chunks of ginger and dark vinegar. These soups have cleansing qualities, especially for the new mother. In return, our guests gave money in small red envelopes to wish Vickie long life and happiness. Several remarked how nice and round Vickie's face was and how porcelain-white her skin was, a sign of beauty. For years Mom compared my skin coloring with that of my friends. "But Mom," I argued, "Those friends look pale and sickly. Dark skin is a healthier look." My words fell on deaf ears. Now people use tanning machines and sprays at salons and spas, and I suppose that is a lot less harmful than basking directly in the sun for a tan.

Mom placed a 24 karat gold chain with a jade pendant around Vickie's neck. This would ward off evil and keep Vickie calm and serene. Mom lost her big tummy, which she blamed on gas and sewing. I guess she passed her gas, but she did not give up sewing. A few weeks later we bundled Vickie up in blankets and took her to DeFremery Park. My sisters and I raced to see who could climb the jungle gym the fastest. Next, I ran for the swings. Then we dashed to the metal "go-round saucer," grabbed the bars and ran to spin the base as fast as we could before jumping on for a joy ride until we spun out of control or became dizzy. What a time we had! It did not matter that we had our Sunday best on. We finally settled down when Mom walked us across the street and had us pose in front of the Juvenile Hall for pictures.

Vickie's arrival added more chores for my sisters and me, which included feeding and carrying her and washing diapers. I stood tip-toed on a wooden crate to reach the faucets of the concrete tubs anchored outside on the back porch. The water from the "COLD" water tap was icy cold, as was the water from the faucet marked "HOT." Using a wood-and-metal washboard, I scrubbed and wrung out the wash until my knuckles turned white. On blustery days, the laundry we hung on the clotheslines simulated ghosts dancing in the wind. For months there was a stench at one corner of the yard near the clotheslines. Finally Mom paid a plumber to fix the broken sewer pipe, but not before I accidentally stepped into the large pool of brown glop hidden by knee-high weeds. My missteps left coin-sized stains on my socks as the sewage oozed up through the holes on the bottom of my shoes.

By now Mom had already taught us older girls to cook. Every night we cooked rice on top of the old gas stove, using a short matchstick from a tin box to light the burner. Every fourth day was my turn to make dinner. Making rice was a challenge. Once the pot of rice came to a full boil, it was a game to lift the lid before the rice boiled over. When the water boiled down, I then lowered the flames to let the rice finish steaming. Nothing was worse than a pot of burnt rice except a gooey mess on the stove. I learned to use a heavy cleaver, even though I could barely grip the fat wooden handle. I sliced and stir-fried flank steak with onions. I flattened cloves of garlic with the sides of the cleaver so that the garlic skin peeled off easily, but that left a scent on my fingers that would not easily wash away. I scaled fresh rock codfish and steamed it with slivers of raw ginger and slices of black mushrooms, sealing the flavor with a spoonful of hot oil. The hardest thing to chop was a chunk of raw pork butt until it was soft enough to mold into a large meat patty, which was then steamed with preserved greens or salted fish. I stood on tip-toes with my narrow shoulders suspended over the meat like the spread of an eagle's wings hovering over its prey. Chomp, chomp. Each time the cleaver hit the old wooden chopping block, it resonated. Our neighbors must have wondered what I was killing in the kitchen. The dip and discoloration in the center of the chopping block revealed years of use, and it made me wonder where the slivers of wood went. Did I swallow any of them?

Mom told me the story about when her friends who worked with her in San Francisco dropped in for a visit. When it was time to serve dinner to our company, Mom went into the kitchen to cut the whole chicken into serving pieces, but I had already chopped it and placed the pieces neatly on a serving dish in the shape of a whole chicken, without telling her. She was shocked and very proud of the job I had done, for being just thirteen years old.

When Mom suffered severe headaches, we seared thin slices of fresh ginger root over an open flame at the stove and placed the hot pieces across her forehead, securing them with a scarf knotted at the back of her head. When her back ached, we took turns pounding between her shoulder blades with our fists to draw the "poison" out. I stopped when the spots turned purple, but I could not stop just because my arms tired. Often I could smell Tiger Balm, White Flower Oil, homemade whisky rub, Vick's VapoRub, Ben Gay ointment, or mustard patches and knew Mom was having a bad day with her many aches and pains.

A certain spot in the backyard was where my sisters and I took turns performing another chore: burning trash, dried weeds and old newspapers in a rusty thirty-gallon drum. No permits were needed from the fire department to do this at home. I took great care in knowing when to fuel the fire with more trash before it died and how much to add without the flames flaring up in my face. I loved watching the red glow of the embers, mesmerized as the sparks flickered in the air while I used a long tree branch to jab and stab at the hot gray-and-white ashes. On cold days, I felt the warmth from the flames, like people gathered around a campfire roasting marshmallows. But no matter how hard I tried to dodge the smoke that kept drifting toward me, I smelled of smoke as I went back into the house.

As we got older, Mom sent us off on errands to buy things on sale. She seemed to know where the bargains were: up the ramp to the second floor of Swan's Tenth Street Market for cans of tuna fish, Sixth Street Housewife's Market for dried apricots, and H. C. Capwell's bargain basement on Twentieth and Broadway for "back-to-school" sales at the end of each August. Mom sent us to Simon's Hardware on Eighth and Broadway, Kress's Five and Dime on Fourteenth and Broadway for hot dogs with tomato catsup and mustard, Penney's on Tenth and Washington, and the old Payless Drug Store on Telegraph and Eighteenth. On my own I would buy a few lemon drops or a small bag of Spanish peanuts. For shoes we went to Leed's, Burt's, or Chandler's on Washington Street, where I bought a pair of lavender flats and a small square black leather bullet purse. We could not afford to shop at the better stores like Kahn's on Telegraph, nor Roos-Atkins or Kushin's on Broadway. Of course Mom sent us to buy Chinese food in Chinatown: Quong On Teong, Sang Cheong, Man Lung, Yet Sun and Lun Kee, whose owner's wife shared food with Mom on Angel Island. We shopped at Ninth Street Market, where freshly butchered chickens still thrashed in garbage cans. We walked everywhere. We walked so much it made the holes on the bottom of my shoes bigger. We were sweaty and exhausted by the time we made it home with our shopping list done.

If Mom came shopping with us, the first thing she did when we arrived home was kick off her shoes, pull off her clingy nylon stockings, and remove the garter belt that held them. But mostly Mom stayed home to sew. For a period of time, Mom tried to teach us to read and write Chinese. She would stop her sewing and gather us around a table to teach our lessons, but when we did not catch on fast enough, she stopped. I wish now she had made us learn to read and write Chinese. She taught us how to play *Mah Jong*, a wonderful game like gin rummy; for years Mom played every weekend with two different sets of friends, playing like a pro but finally giving up the game when she felt she was winning much too often.

On days I did not cook, I rotated to other chores like washing dishes, cleaning house, sweeping the hall and porch, hoeing weeds, picking tomatoes and zucchini from our vegetable garden and doing laundry. When I complained about one of my sisters not taking her turn to do a certain chore, Mom said, "Do it for me. Each thing you do is one thing less I have to stop and do myself. Please." We should help. After all, Mom worked hard and was tired. I understand that now. Good thing there were several of us to share the work, and it did not all fall on any one sister's shoulder, except maybe Marilyn's.

Six months after Vickie was born, another emergency call was made to the doctor. This time it was for my father, who had been ill for many years. The doctor admitted him into a hospital about a two-hour drive away in a town near San Jose. Dad remained there for ten years. How Mom persevered, I do not know, but more on this in a later chapter.

ACROSS THE OCEAN

She sailed across the ocean
When she was twenty-five
On the USS Coolidge
In nineteen thirty-five

In her hand she clenched a photo
Of a stranger she was to marry
Arranged to be his future bride
A promise she vowed to carry

She arrived at Angel Island
Just across the bay
From the land of Gum San, Gold Mountain
Soon she will be on her way

She spoke not a word of English
Detained and interrogated
By government authorities
Like an enemy hated

There were others like her
Locked up like criminals
Not free to roam the island
Locked up like animals

Two months later
The guards unlocked the door
She was released and turned over
To relatives on the shore

He came across the ocean
How I do not know
Like her he came from China
When I do not know

They got married to each other
Quickly settled down
They lived in a tiny apartment
Near Grant Avenue Chinatown

Mom gave birth to four daughters
One right after another
We were about a year apart
Sadly none was a brother

Mom learned to sew
She sewed night and day
Just to feed and clothe us
And keep us out of harm's way

World War II broke out
In nineteen forty-two
Young men marched off to war
Women joined them too

When the war was over
Not all soldiers came home
Many of them died fighting
For those of us at home

Then another girl was born
Now I was third of five
What was Mom to do with us
Just to keep us alive

Now I do appreciate my mom
For giving birth to me
Without her I would not be here
Had she not crossed the sea

CHAPTER TEN:

THE GOOD TIMES

With Vickie's arrival, my sisters and I had more work to do and little time to play. We did not have toys. The one doll we shared in San Francisco was a 1942 Shirley Temple doll, which broke before our move to Oakland. One time Dad came home with four dolls he bought for ten dollars. Though Mom felt they could not afford the price of $2.50 each, she did not fault him because he was, for a change, thinking of his girls.

In Oakland, we sisters shared a two-story aluminum doll house that opened in the back for us to play "house" with our tiny two-inch pink plastic dolls with loose arms and legs that swiveled so they could not stay sitting without falling back or flat on their faces. Still, we had fun with those little dolls. We had less time to play with our small celadon green celluloid toy dishes, but when we did, we took turns playing waitress and passing out homemade menus. We sat at our small white wooden table, and picked up the tiny teacups delicately with our thumb and index fingers. "And what are you having today?" I asked one of my sisters as I pulled a short pencil from behind my ear and turned a page of my home-made order pad. I flipped my short, straight hair with one hand, turned my face to one side, blinked my eyes slowly, and pointed my nose up toward the ceiling. We were so sophisticated!

Marilyn, who enjoyed reading, took us to the main library at Fourteenth and Clay Street, across from the ice rink that later became a fire station. We carried stacks of books home to read until our arms were nearly broken—books like Johanna Spyri's "Heidi," Maud Hart Lovelace's "Betsy, Tacy and Tib," wonderfully illustrated by Lois Lenski, and Louisa May Alcott's "Little Women." I pretended I was one of the four Little Women: Meg, Jo, Amy or Beth, and in the movie by the same title, my favorite actress was Margaret O'Brien, because she was sweet, delicate and fragile. We drew and cut out paper dolls. We read the Sunday "Aunt Elsie's" column, which featured stories, poems and drawings sent in by schoolchildren. I wanted to see my name in print too, but had no idea how to submit a drawing, let alone obtain a three cent stamp. We knelt on the sofa in the living room and looked out the windows to watch the streetcars. We played a game to see who could quickly name the passing cars—Ford, Hudson, Nash, Plymouth, Buick, DeSoto and Pontiac. It was easy to recognize Buicks with the three classic exhaust holes on each side.

As we became older, Mom took a job downtown sewing nightgowns at Little Lady's at the corner of Twelve and Harrison. She enjoyed the company of my great-aunt *Goo Por*, who helped Mom get the job. When Mom came home after work each day, we huddled around the radio and listened to "The Lone Ranger," "Amos and Andy," and "My Friend Bill." I was in awe, as I thought the characters really talked and lived inside the radio. What miracles electricity could transmit!

One day, a friend told Mom, "Penney's in downtown Oakland is going out of business, and everything is on sale. I picked up six nice dresses in different sizes for one dollar each and you may buy them from me for your daughters if you'd like. There is no obligation." Mom had the money and was delighted she was asked. Of course she wanted them for her girls.

With the advent of black-and-white television in the early

1950s, Marilyn, with a job living and working outside of our home, contributed $100, along with Mom's $100, toward the purchase of a TV, so we were one of the first to own a TV in our neighborhood. *Bok Moo* at the corner store was envious. We glued ourselves to the screen and watched comedy acts and variety shows on one of three channels: ABC, NBC, or CBS. Each week we roared to tears watching Milton Berle, Red Skelton, Jackie Gleason, Bob Hope, Eddie Cantor, George Burns and Gracie Allen, Sid Caesar and Imogene Coca, Danny Thomas, Dean Martin, Jerry Lewis, Martha Raye, Lucille Ball and "forever 39" deadpan Jack Benny. We were mesmerized for hours over the Lone Ranger, Hopalong Cassidy, the Cisco Kid and Pancho and Gene Autry as they cracked their whips and rode their horses faster than the wind. Roy Rogers and Dale Evans ended each week singing "Happy Trails to You..." "Your Hit Parade" with Dorothy Collins, Gisele MacKenzie, Snooky Lanson and Russell Arms presented the top seven pop tunes each week. Without doing a single thing, Loretta Young and Bess Myerson both looked ravishing, while Dinah Shore smacked her "Um Wah" goodbyes for Chevrolet. Art Linkletter, Howdy Doody and Crusader Rabbit were many kids' favorites, as well as mine. My other favorite programs were "I Remember Mama," "My Friend Irma (Wilson)" and tall, thin, stone-faced Arthur Murray, dashing into view in a black tuxedo with long tails, teaching ballroom dance lessons along with his petite brunette wife.

All summer long we watched TV matinees on "Golden Gate Playhouse" as I sat on my favorite spot on the sofa and ate egg salad or tuna sandwiches for lunch. If there was nothing else, we sprinkled sugar on two slices of white bread, or I sucked on a whole lemon. We watched television only after we rushed through our chores in the morning, which by now included hoeing the knee-high weeds and tending the vegetable plants in our front yard. When we got a bumper crop of tomatoes, we sold them to *Bok Moo* for a dollar a case. *Bok Moo* preferred them green, which she stir-fried with beef, and sold the rest to her customers.

Muriel and I shared the duplex bed while Joanne and Marilyn slept on the other two sofas in the living room. Vickie shared the bedroom with Mom and Dad. I read comic books late into the night, straining to make out Donald Duck and his nephews, Huey, Dewey and Louie; L'il Abner and Daisy Mae; Archie; Dagwood; Little Lulu, with black curly hair; Nancy and Tubby; and Little Orphan Annie with the bright red curly hair and haunting black eyes. Even after Mom yelled from her room, "Stop reading or you'll go blind," I continued to read under the sheets until I finally gave up squinting at the words.

When we first moved to Oakland, Mom took us on the train to San Francisco on the weekends so that we could continue seeing Chinese movies. Eventually we stopped going to San Francisco and went to the matinee movies at the small neighborhood theater at Fourteenth and Peralta streets. Each week I was glad to settle into our seats to watch the lavish American made-in-color Hollywood musicals featuring handsome actors, partnered with beautiful blond-haired, blue-eyed actresses clad in long, flowing chiffon gowns trimmed with satin bows and feathers. They sang and danced in opulent style, gliding down long curved staircases. They waltzed across marble-tiled floors with chandeliers high above their heads. They were the likes of Fred Astaire, Ginger Rogers, Gene Kelly, Doris Day, Donald O'Connor, Jane Powell, Van Johnson and Debbie Reynolds. Even young, dimpled-cheek actress Shirley Temple, pouting and frowning with a head full of ringlets, tap-danced down the staircase with her butler. Mom would never let us frown like that. "Not pretty," she often reminded us, "and those lines will become permanent on your foreheads." I remember someone had a collection of 8-x-10 black and white glossy photographs of Shirley Temple, each one autographed, like for a fan club member, and probably worth a lot today. I spent hours looking at these until one day they just disappeared! Maybe they were only on loan to us, but Shirley was cute even when she puckered her lips and frowned.

When we walked home from the movie theater, we passed right by The Sunshine Market, a little grocery store on Adeline, where Mom (by no means a gambler), when she had an extra dime, sent us to buy a Chinese Lottery ticket in hopes of winning money. As I looked up at a billboard advertising Sunbeam Bread, I wondered why I did not have curly blond hair piled high on my head like the little girl in the ad, who wore a blue-and-white-checked dress on the bread label, and I wondered why I did not live like "real people do" as in the movies, singing and dancing and having a good time.

When better movies played downtown, Mom sent us to the fancy Fox Theater at Eighteenth and Telegraph, the Central, and the lavish art deco Paramount Theater on Broadway, or the Roxie Theater on Seventeenth Street. My sisters and I took turns carrying Vickie for blocks until our arms and legs gave out. Sometimes Mom took a break from sewing and accompanied us to Lake Merritt, a lovely man-made landmark in the heart of Oakland, to enjoy the warmth of the sun and fresh air. While Mom napped on the lawn, we ran barefooted in circles around her, chasing and laughing quietly so as not to awaken her. I liked the feel of the blades of grass tickling the bottoms of my feet.

Each July Fourth, we found a great spot early in the morning to park our blankets at Lake Merritt to watch the sailboats and speedboats vie for prizes. Within hours, the park filled with people who came from all directions. When the sun went down, beautiful fireworks filled the sky with rainbow colors seen for miles. It was magical, seeing the sparks of confetti in an array of colors—reds, yellows, oranges, blues, greens, purples—flickering and cascading down before fizzling into the water so close to us. I could almost touch them. However, after several boat and firework accidents and the cost of putting on the show, the City of Oakland was forced to halt the special holiday events. The magic was gone, forever… as was a magical part of my childhood.

CHAPTER ELEVEN:

NO TIME FOR GOODBYES

Now I bring you to June 1952 when as a thirteen-year-old, I stood at the curb in front of our house in West Oakland with my worldly possessions in a crumbled, brown paper bag (in place of a suitcase) at my feet, waiting and watching for a stranger to come take me away. I wanted to say goodbye to someone, anyone. As I turned around and glanced back at the old, weathered front door, neither my mom nor any of my sisters emerged on the porch to wave or say goodbye. I stood there alone and wondered if I would be missed. There were no discussions as to why I needed to go, or whether I wanted to go or not. I was angry, confused and hurt, but I did not cry.

I had never been away from home except once when I stayed overnight with my oldest sister Marilyn at my great-aunt *Goo Por's* beautiful house on Mandana Boulevard in the Upper Lakeshore District of East Oakland—the time when her daughter Bess, now married to an optometrist, Dr. Clayton Soohoo, dropped us off to see Walt Disney's *Fantasia* at the Grand Lake Theater. Marilyn, being the oldest, was the first to leave home at thirteen to work in Piedmont with a family that had three young children. Frustrated with the very demanding job, she left to work for an older couple with adult children who were on their own. She earned twenty-five dollars a month; of that, she gave fifteen dollars to Mom to help pay bills. Two years after Marilyn started, Joanne, the second-born and one year older than I, went to live and work with a couple not far from where Marilyn worked. Now it was my turn to follow in the footsteps of my two older sisters: to leave home, move in with a white family and work. I was no exception. I wonder if this new family would be nice to me or work me to death.

Rich white families in Piedmont, an affluent city next to Oakland, hired young Asian students to cook, clean, wash, iron, and babysit in exchange for room, board and a small paycheck. Typically these year-round after-school jobs, classified as "mother's helpers," continued full-time at summer vacation homes throughout California in places such as Lake Tahoe and cities in Southern California. Through either a referral from one of my sisters or someone at school, I landed a job with Mrs. Landers, who interviewed me over the phone. She needed help with her four grandchildren who were spending several weeks of the summer at her cabin in Lake Tahoe.

Finally Mrs. Landers, a woman in her mid-40s or 50s, pulled up to the curb in what one would call a "gas guzzler," and we headed northeast to Lake Tahoe with her four grandchildren: three boys and a girl who ranged in ages from one to nine. The day started sunny and warm and temperatures climbed as we drove through Sacramento in what seemed well over ninety-degree heat. My clothes stuck to me while streams of sweat trickled down my forehead and neck. Air-conditioning meant hand-cranking down the car windows so that everyone's hair blew in their faces—instant gratification that lasted for only a few minutes. The children's moaning, whining, teasing, poking and jabbing at each other were uncontrollable no matter how many times Mrs. Landers handed out treats and told them to stop.

"Grandma, he hit me," said one.

"She kicked me first," cried another.

"He took my window seat," piped up yet another one.

"You all stop it right now," demanded Mrs. Landers to no

avail as she tried to concentrate on her driving. The children climbed and switched from the front seats to the back, kicking, nudging and bumping into me and I ended up most of the time squashed in the middle of the back seat carrying the baby boy on my lap with our arms stuck to each other with sweat. As the children grew more rambunctious, I knew I was in trouble for the summer. How will these kids behave and listen to me when they won't even listen to their grandmother? I bet they would behave had their parents been with us, but they weren't. Finally the last child drifted off to sleep. I thought to myself, if I ever have kids, mine would be quiet, well-behaved and most of all respectful like I was taught. Their misbehavior reminded me of the times when my sisters and I argued with each other or tried to back-talk. Mom would not tolerate the verbal abuse and clamor, "Now stop it. Remember, what you do or say will come back to you when you have kids of your own. You'll see." Just the thought of that happening to me was enough to make me heed her warnings. I glanced over at each child, sweet and angelic for now, and nodded.

Soon we passed clumps of late May snowfall melting alongside the road. Tall evergreens dwarfed the winding road as the sun dodged between the branches and the trees, blinding my eyes like exploding flashbulbs. We had been on the road for several hours straight, except for a few pit stops including one for lunch. Mrs. Landers' driving became erratic as the path narrowed and we climbed higher elevations indicated by the markers I read along the road. I cringed when she swerved across the imaginary double yellow lines but felt relieved every time she pulled over to let a stream of vehicles, trucks and semis pass. I closed my eyes to keep from seeing the long drop over the cliffs' edges to the roaring stream below, and though I needed a nap, I dared not fall asleep.

We headed east toward Soda Springs and as we arrived at The Cedars, a private camp of family cabins, I took a deep breath and was in awe as we came to a stop at a lovely woodsy setting. Pine cones up to twelve inches long littered the ground, the air was fresh and crisp, and a short distance away, birds chirped their love songs. I heard water trickling from a nearby brook, like dancing water… a pleasant sound I was to hear throughout the night from my room. Dirt paths connected each isolated cabin to the main road. There were no electricity or heat and everything ran on portable tanks of "Flamo" gas. At night we lit portable gas lanterns, which we carried from room to room. The one-story rustic cabin was built on a foundation slightly above ground with a wooden deck completely encircling the building. Each room had a door that led directly out onto the deck. Night air dropped to freezing temperatures and tales abounded of bears and wolves that lurked outside around the garbage cans searching for food. The last thing I did every night was reach up to turn off the lantern hanging from my bedpost before curling up under the cold covers. As lights went out for everyone, I was surrounded by total darkness except for the moon casting strange shapes of light and dark shadows through the uncovered window panes. I wished I was home.

Early each morning at the crack of dawn, everyone yelled, "Oh, Joe!" which echoed across the camp floor. It was the daily wake-up call for breakfast at the community dining hall. I stayed behind to feed and care for the baby and did not join the family for any of the meals or activities at the center although I wanted to. All day long I heard the din of voices and laughter from a distance like the sound of children playing in the school yard during recess. A few weeks later, the children's mother, with a round face, short brown curly hair and wearing glasses, arrived with their German Shepherd, which made my hair stand on end since I was afraid of dogs and cats. One time the dog took off after a porcupine and came pouncing back whimpering and bleeding with his mouth full of quills. It was painful for me to stand and watch each quill being pulled and removed though it was done as gently and carefully as possible. Another time he went after a skunk… good thing that one got away!

At summer's end, the kid's mom drove back to Southern California with them as Mrs. Landers and I headed back to the Bay Area. For lunch she stopped at a popular roadside restaurant and I could order whatever I wanted from the menu, so I ate a juicy "bloody rare" hamburger with all the fixings and delicious French fries. We sat at a table by the window with a magnificent view of the breathtaking mountains behind us and for me eating out at a nice American restaurant was a new experience. Arriving at home, there were no warm welcomes or expressions of anyone missing me while I was gone, but I was very glad to be home and back in my own bed.

In December, I received a dark blue customized card from the children's mom, with silver embossed lettering under the silhouettes naming each of the family members, including their pet dog and cat. I cherished this unusual card with the raised letters because someone thought enough of me during the holidays to send me a greeting. Their card reminded me of the time Joanne and I went door-to-door in our West Oakland neighborhood with a catalog and tried to sell Christmas cards. We canvassed blocks upon blocks of homes and businesses and had no sale until a real estate agent on Market Street placed an order for some expensive cards with personalized engraving. Maybe he liked our sales pitch or saw the plea of desperation in our eyes, but whatever his reason I was thrilled because the sale was the first time I had earned money. Oh how I wish I still kept that card from the family that did not work me to death.

For the past two years I attended seventh and eighth grades at Westlake Junior High School on Harrison Street above Grand Avenue by Lake Merritt, using great-aunt *Goo Por's* address on Mandana Boulevard because West Oakland was outside the boundaries of Westlake, one of the best junior highs, we thought, in Oakland. I looked forward to returning in the spring of 1953 as a high and mighty ninth-grade senior. Only senior girls wore white middy blouses with starched sailor collars and navy pleated wool skirts for special events, and only the smart ones stood out like my sister Joanne wearing her tiny silver, and gold, "W" honor pins on the knot of her navy blue tie. I wanted the chance to earn my honor pins too! I also looked forward to meeting the crop of Chinese students transferring from Lincoln Elementary School in Chinatown because that school went only up to the eighth grade. After a year at Westlake, those students would be moving on to different high schools like Oakland Technical High or Oakland High. I heard how much fun outgoing and friendly Joanne had with her Westlake graduating class before she left for Oakland High and I wanted that same experience – though in a shy way.

Mrs. Tusher, my counselor and art teacher, who had curly shoulder-length brown hair and wore angora and cashmere pull-over sweaters and cardigans that showed her shapely curves, was my favorite teacher. I often stayed after school to help her clean her classroom, and at the end of the semester she gave me first choice of the old and used art supplies she was tossing out.

On the last day of school before our semester break in 1952, my younger sister Muriel stayed after school to help one of her teachers at Westlake. When the day became dark and rainy, her teacher insisted on driving Muriel home. Arriving at Mandana Boulevard with no keys to the house and no one at home to let Muriel in, she confessed it was not where she lived and directed her to our home in West Oakland. Realizing Muriel did not live in the correct school district, her teacher threatened to report her to the school authorities for using a false address. When Muriel told us what happened, we knew we could be in big trouble, yet we were hopeful that her teacher would have the heart not to turn us in.

Receiving no contact or official word from school during the semester break regarding our status, Muriel and I, somewhat relieved, traipsed off to Westlake for our first day of the new school term in January, ninth grade for me and eighth grade for Muriel. Joanne who was in tenth grade and Marilyn, a senior, were already enrolled at Oakland High using the Mandana address and were not affected by the report.

I listened and observed as the teacher in each of my classrooms called out the names of the new Chinese students. Tommy Chinn and Clifford Lew seemed like nice guys. I heard that Carol Louie, tiny and petite like me, was very smart. Checking first to see what she looked like, I secretly planned to stick with her in my college prep courses: English, Spanish, Algebra, and Biology, with Physical Education (P.E.) and Home Economics (Home Econ.) rounding out the rest of my classes.

On the second day of school, Muriel and I were called into the Principal's office and I knew he had bad news for us. We were told to leave Westlake immediately and report the following morning to Prescott Junior High on Campbell Street in West Oakland. I was devastated and heartbroken. How would I explain this to the girls I had known since seventh grade: Carole, class comic Arlene, Lois, Deanne who played the piano in orchestra, Barbara, Patty, Marlene, and the pretty twins, Olivia and Jeanne? These were the girls who befriended me. And what about the boys: Bucky, student leader Dick, Merv, curly blond Ronnie whom I knew in grammar school, and the two class cut-ups, Stan and Al? Oh, how Arlene, Stan and Al could put together skits at the school assemblies and had the student body rolling in the aisles with laughter when the trio sang their rendition of songs like "Yabba Dabba Honeymoon" or "C'mon a My House."

What would I say to the friends I just met? How will I say goodbye to them? If they do not see me in class tomorrow, will they wonder why?

Muriel and I had barely enough time to clear our desks and hall lockers. I headed for the girls' gym and from my locker I grabbed my P.E. uniform—the two-piece blue button-down, short-sleeved shirt and matching bloomer shorts with the elastic leg bands. Our stern P.E. teacher, Mrs. Neal with the short curly reddish-brown hair, made sure we labeled the shirt pocket and waistband with our first initials and last names for identity. I was proud of the neat job I did hand-embroidering my name in block letters with white thread. Mrs. Neal also checked that our outfits were taken home every Friday and laundered, but often running short of time, I merely ironed and brought them back to school on Monday like they were clean and washed. If Mrs. Neal detected they were not, the demerit points I would receive could lower my P.E. grade.

Leaving Westlake meant I would lose my cashiering job in the student cafeteria, where I was compensated with free lunches that included my choice of chocolate pudding, tapioca or Jello cubes with a glob of whipped cream… desserts I never ate at home. Leaving Westlake also meant I would not have another opportunity to be in Miss Louise Jorgensen's Christmas Pageant at the Oakland Auditorium. Once a famous ballerina, Miss Jorgensen was the sole director and choreographer of the program and went from school to school to audition and select nearly 1600 students to dance parts in the annual event. I was in the "Light" number, a ballet number danced to one of the famous classical "Nutcracker" pieces, wearing a ballerina-length dress with layers of net skirts. We were clustered by groups wearing pastel colors of pink, yellow, light green, baby blue or lavender. I loved pointing my toes as we jete'ed and arabesqued across the huge auditorium floor. I envied the elite dancers from the "Dance Workshop" who were given special parts to perform. There were many other wonderful numbers with dolls, toy soldiers, snow men and women, candy sticks, reindeers and elves performed by students from other schools throughout Oakland. For the finale each year hundreds of tiny, adorable kindergarten "fairies" all dressed in white dresses and anklets skipped out onto the center of the huge auditorium floor and surrounded Miss Jorgensen, with the spotlight on her in the middle holding the magic wand as the "Spirit of Christmas," a role she portrayed in the pageant for 62 years. I looked forward to being picked again next year for another performance, but these hopes were now gone.

I would miss the wonderful French fries smothered with gobs of French mustard I used to buy after school at a tiny Mom-and-Pop store a couple of blocks up toward Harrison and Frisbie Street, where Deanne lived, before walking home or running for a bus on Grand Avenue. I would not be earning my silver and gold "W" pins for scholastic achievement or a block "W" for participating in before-and-after-school sports. I would not have a chance to become Carol's friend.

The next morning as we did every morning, Muriel and I walked our 4-1/2 year old sister Vickie to St. Vincent's Day Care, once a beautiful Victorian house, on Eighth and Chestnut Streets. The Catholic nuns in long black habits were very fond of Vickie. One time when she was about three, wearing a two-piece red Chinese satin pant outfit, Vickie sang "Me and My Teddy Bear" at a special performance and brought the house down as she performed with her cuddly teddy bear. After bidding Vickie goodbye, Muriel and I headed to Prescott going in an opposite direction from the one we used to take to Westlake. I was so distraught I had nothing to say.

Though the teachers seem nice enough, going to my new school was not the same as going to Westlake. In my homemaking class at Prescott, there were no sewing machines. In contrast, Westlake had a whole row of Singers under the tall windows along one wall plus large cutting tables where we laid out the paper patterns on our fabric. The lady teacher at Prescott pulled out a bag of yarn and taught us how to knit with big wooden needles about size 13. It did not take me long to knit and purl a long wool scarf. Lunch time in the student cafeteria was noisy and disorderly, but Muriel and I qualified for the free lunch program without signing up for it. The best part was I did not have to work for my free lunches.

I really missed Westlake. I cried and cried silently to myself, but nothing could stop the hurt, and I wished Mom or Marilyn could do something to get Muriel and me out of Prescott.

CHAPTER TWELVE:

EAST OAKLAND

Spring 1953. What a headache for Mom. She was raising five girls (Vickie the youngest was only four years old) and trying to hold down her sewing job; Marilyn and Joanne were away from home, except for their days off, and Muriel and I were expelled from Westlake.

Mom must have sensed Muriel and I were unhappy having to change schools and knew she had to do something for us. She instructed Marilyn to buy a copy of the local newspaper and flip to the real estate section for homes on sale in East Oakland, a good neighborhood. From an ad, they contacted a real estate agent, and because not many families had cars in those days, the agent picked up Marilyn and Mom and drove them to several of the listings.

On April 16, Mom purchased from Mr. Denton a two-story, single-family converted duplex for $12,500 at 1528 Eighth Avenue, between East Fifteenth and Foothill Boulevard in the Oakland High School District, which included the ninth grade at that time. Next door was a three-story apartment building with a china and glass foundry on the ground floor. Every time I passed by the front of the shop, it smelled like machinery oil burning. At the end of the block on the corner of Foothill was a large apartment building with four adjoining retail store fronts named the Oakland China Studio, which displayed exquisite table settings of colorful porcelain dishes (supplied by the foundry around the corner), tall crystal water goblets, glass and silver candle holders, and fancy silver and gold flatware. I loved looking through the large windows at the dining room furniture and the formal place settings. On the other side of our house was the Elim Tabernacle Church. The church was later sold to a Southern Baptist group. On the front of our house were rose bushes, a short, neatly trimmed hedge, and a lumpy lawn that Vickie claimed she mowed for years beautified the front of our house. Along one side of the lawn was a tall hedge that bordered the long gravel driveway to the three dilapidated detached garages in the backyard.

In the living room, a gas heater sat in front of a defunct fireplace. When the heater was in use, which was not often, Mom kept a teakettle filled with water on top of it to keep the air from drying up in the room. A dark green, boxy-shaped sofa covered in a tight chenille material, a matching arm chair, a blond rectangular coffee table, two end tables, and a television set that Marilyn helped purchase completed the furnishings in the room. We used to chase Vickie around the coffee table when Mom was away at work at Little Lady's. One time when Vickie was acting bratty, we threatened her. "If you don't behave, we are going to call the police to take you away." At that very instant, we heard the sirens of a passing ambulance blare in front of our house. "See, here they come to take you away to jail!" we teased. Poor Vickie went into hysterics and was never the same after that! She was outnumbered by her older siblings, and no one came to her defense. Alas, life is not always fair!

Two tall wooden sliding doors separated one end of the living room from the dining room; we kept those doors closed when company came so no one could see that we used the dining room as a bedroom for my three sisters. Part of the time, I slept on the green sofa in the living room. Past the dining room was Mom's and Vickie's bedroom, with a small closet. A door beyond that led into a small, narrow bathroom with a bathtub on legs, a toilet, and a wash basin. Over the wash basin was a built-in wooden medicine cabinet and mirror that had so many coats of paint, the door would not shut tight.

A large kitchen adjoined the bathroom, with a small hall and a swinging door that led back into the dining room. An old gas stove, a white sink, a water heater that never supplied enough hot water for us, and a gray chrome dinette set with six matching chairs covered in gray naugahyde barely filled the spacious kitchen. The woodwork was painted off-white—"offu-white," as Mom would say with her accent… which sounded awful.

Under the stairwell was a small, dingy room with a low slanted ceiling and a tiny closet where we stuffed our clothes. The room had been wallpapered by the previous occupant with old *National Geographic* maps of the world in color; they had yellowed over the years, leaving the corners of the maps curled and peeling off the walls. Mom's heavy sewing machine (she no longer sewed at home) took up nearly all the floor space, but by now my sisters and I had learned to sew at school and made simple skirts and dresses at home using Mom's machine. We added a small, narrow rolltop oak desk and an old Royal manual typewriter. Eventually this became the study room where I banged out many essays and term papers for school.

Past the kitchen was a small, bright and sunny back room with a washtub and a door to a small back porch, where we stood to hang out the laundry with wooden clothespins on a clothesline connected by pulleys to a long pole at the end of our back yard. Shortly after we moved in, Mom bought a modern washing machine; it had a round tub with a wringer that we hand-cranked to expel excess water from the wash. I no longer had to stand on tiptoes in the freezing cold to do laundry outside in a concrete tub.

A thin albino woman with a blond bobbed haircut lived in the upstairs flat with her adult daughter and son. A set of wooden stairs on one side of the house connected them to their own outside entrance. They were quiet and friendly and remained Mom's reliable tenants, which meant more rent for Mom to collect, besides the monthly rental income she continued to receive from keeping our Sixteenth Street place. We moved into the spacious, one-bedroom bottom flat—six females and no male.

I transferred mid-semester to Oakland High School, located at Park and MacArthur Boulevards. What a relief it was not to have to use a fake address! This school became my third ninth-grade school in three months, and I hoped I could adjust to my classes. It was not easy stepping into a new school and class in the middle of the semester. My biggest worry was, who would I eat lunch with every day? I missed my friends at Westlake. Now I knew how children of military parents must feel when they get reassigned every so many years and relocate to new homes, schools, cities, sometimes even foreign countries.

In spite of its grand ornate architectural design, depending on how one looked at it, students referred to Oakland High, which was built in 1928, as either the "Pink Palace" or the "Pink Prison" because of its pale stucco color and Neo-Gothic architecture. Muriel enrolled in eighth grade at Roosevelt Junior High on Nineteenth Avenue. Vickie went to preschool at Bella Vista Elementary on East 28th Street and Tenth Avenue, and later to kindergarten at Franklin Elementary School, a couple of blocks from home. Marilyn and Joanne, still living and working as "mother's helpers" with the same families in Piedmont, were already attending Oakland High.

Whenever I passed my sisters in the halls at Oakland High, we acknowledged each other by merely nodding, with little or no conversation until they came home on their days off. In a sense, we were like strangers, since we did not live together. Today our family would be described as "dysfunctional," and Mom would be classified as a "single mom," both labels not familiar to me in those days.

With a total enrollment of over 2,000 students at Oakland High, the student body was divided into two lunch periods.

On the first day of school, I was relieved to find Marilyn, now a mighty senior, in the cafeteria with her friends, Velma Dong and Edna Saunders, and a couple of other classmates. I joined them at their table, hoping they did not mind, happy I did not have to eat alone. Joanne was assigned a different time slot and had already established her own group of friends to eat with.

I found it very difficult to make new friends—especially in the middle of the semester, when cliques had already formed and lunch groups established. It was not until the following year in tenth grade that two girls in my class invited me to join in their lunch partnership: Edith Eggert, who came from Bret Harte Junior High, and Jean Krauskopf, who lived on East 15th Street, around the corner from our house. Her house was the one with the French Laundry sign in front, though she was German.

Most ninth graders came to Oakland High from McChesney Junior High, where a small number of the white girls belonged to secret sororities and wore expensive Tyrolean print dresses with the Lanz label. Years later I heard from a woman who lived in my retirement community that when she really wanted to be in the sorority with her close friends, she was rejected because she did not have enough cashmere sweaters and did not have sex with a high enough number of the boys in school. I do not know how true that was, but anyway I did not have that problem since I was not interested in joining a sorority.

Many of the girls wore layers of crinolines and heavily starched petticoats under their full skirts, and looked like square dancers. My sisters and I made our own petticoats, and one time I made one with a casing at the hem and inserted a heavy wire made out of coat hangers through the casing to make my skirt bellow out. It was nearly impossible to take a seat on the bus or in class because the front of my skirt would flip up and hit me in the face when I sat down. Oh, what one would do to keep up with the fads, and I, of all people, must have looked ridiculous! Tight wool skirts and soft cashmere sweater sets were very popular as well, along with detachable collars called "dickies." I wore my homemade dresses and gathered skirts. Also popular for the girls were the wide, full circle skirts decorated with French poodle appliqués, rhinestones, chains and bows. When Mom saw one for the first time in a store, it was so different and unique that she had to buy one for Vickie. Lucky sister, but I was never envious because mostly not living at home, I was not aware of the things Mom bought for her.

Girls wore their hair in long, wavy curls, ponytails, or short "duck tails." I went to bed with my hair set in pin curls, and in the morning I never knew which way my curls were going to go – either east or west. They had stubborn minds of their own! The guys wore sweaters in our school colors, blue and white, showing off their block "O" earned in school sports, as well as a patch of Willie the Wildcat, Oakland High's mascot. Those who were "in" talked about after-school football games and home parties. I was not among them.

Sandra Percy with the light brown hair and big smile and sweet, demure Lynn Murphy with dark hair welcomed me into the ninth grade chorus class, that is… they spoke to me first. The class was in the midst of rehearsing for the upcoming Spring Sing, an annual event held at the Oakland Auditorium. All the ninth-grade choruses throughout the city practiced at their own individual schools, and then combined for a public evening performance. All those who sang soprano sat together in one section, next to those who sang alto, and so forth. During the one-day rehearsal that preceded the actual performance, I sat in the alto section next to Shirley Yee, one of the students who had transferred from Lincoln to Westlake Junior High, the school I was expelled from. Her parents were the owners of the New Chung King Restaurant at the corner of Tenth and Webster streets. "You were kicked out of school the beginning of this semester?" asked Shirley when I told her I knew some of the students at Westlake. "Yes, I know that teacher. What a shame! You could have been in some of my classes this semester had you remained there." We chatted on and on like we had known each other for years.

No one in my family came to the performance that evening. We harmonized beautifully, and the evening was a success. I thought of the words from one of the songs we sang that night, "You'll Never Walk Alone." *"When you walk through a storm, hold your head up high, and don't be afraid of the dark…"* After the performance I felt alone and afraid as I ran fifteen blocks home in the dark.

I was happy I made a new friend, though she was from another school. Shirley was kind and down-to-earth, and on the night of the Spring Sing, she invited me to play paddle ball the following Saturday at Lincoln Square in Chinatown. No one had ever invited me to anything. I assured her I knew how to get there by bus. One way or another, I will be there! Paddle ball was a game played against a tall wooden backboard, with lines like half of a tennis court drawn on the asphalt. Using wooden paddles, the object was to hit the tennis ball so that the one or two opponents could not keep the ball in play. I aced my balls by hitting them so hard and low that they were not returnable. It was a game of speed, power and strategy, similar to the game of squash, and according to my P.E. teacher I was a whiz at it in school.

On Saturday I took the bus down to Chinatown and met Shirley at the playground. We had barely begun our game when a group of Chinese kids from across the yard who knew Shirley called out to her. They were the usual weekend kids who were forming two softball teams and needed a few more players before picking sides. Sure, why not, *although I would rather beat Shirley in a game of paddle ball.* "Stanley, Stanley, you be captain," someone shouted. "Yeah, you be captain," someone else yelled. A short, thin, nerdy-looking boy stepped forward into the center of the circle. He had a high slanted forehead, long torso, and short legs. He wore a short-sleeve button-down, neatly pressed cotton plaid shirt and dark-rimmed glasses. His high pompadour hairdo, sleeked back above his ears like Elvis, gave him two more inches of height. He grinned proudly. Someone volunteered to be the other captain. The two alternately called out names, picking the muscular guys and the cute, giggly girls first. He looked at me and pointed. I was the last one left, and he did not even ask my name.

I was a good athlete at school, but he would not know that. At Westlake, I played softball and basketball before and after school, earning points toward my block "W" by catching a fly ball or making a basket at the hoop. Mrs. Neal, the P.E. teacher, kept track of these points on her clipboard. On rainy days, when outdoor sports were canceled, she would herd all the students into the gym, slide open the tall wooden accordion doors that separated the girls' gym from the boys' gym, form an inner circle of boys and an outer circle of girls, and teach us the fox trot, pairing everyone with a partner. "Step together forward; step together back," she chanted, and she would repeat this over and over like a drill sergeant as she replayed the record on the old Victrola. I loved learning the dance steps, but every time she stopped the music and shouted, "Change partners," I dreaded getting another nerd with two left feet for my next partner. Mrs. Neal called my sisters and me "The Fongies," and in gym, she gave me a Red A, her equivalent of an A+.

After the softball game with Shirley and her friends, it was time to head home on the bus. Stanley was not impressed that I had played well and helped his team win. I was not impressed with him, either. What made him so popular anyway?

A few weeks later, Shirley called. A classmate of hers was throwing a party at her home in East Oakland. Would I like to come along with her? You bet! It was the first time someone invited me to a party. It was the first time I needed to ask Mom if I could go. I prayed Stanley would not be there. I did not like him and never wanted to see him again…

CHAPTER THIRTEEN:

MOM NEVER SAID GOODBYE

Mom did a wonderful thing by not only getting us out of West Oakland to a better neighborhood and school, but also into a larger house. Time will tell if this move was a good one for us.

Summer 1953 was approaching, and once again it was time for me to look for a summer job, like I had done the previous year when I was thirteen. I found a babysitting job working for Mr. and Mrs. Cross, who had two toddlers. Again I waited at the curb for my ride from a couple I knew only as my new employers. I spent the first night in their Martinez home, about forty miles northeast of Oakland, having no idea how this job would be. The next day we headed to the southern tip of Lake Tahoe. When we arrived at Lower Echo Lake, their close friends, the Dailys, who had their own two toddlers, met us at the parking lot, where we transferred into a speedboat, the only means of getting us through the channel to the rustic cabin at Upper Echo Lake.

The blue water shimmering in the sunlight was clear and beautiful, but I was afraid of sitting so close to the edge of the boat without a life jacket on. Also I did not like my face being kissed by the cold wind and splashed by water. Our boat sped and bounced across the water like a sharp knife cutting through gelatin. Who would save me if the boat tipped over? I closed my eyes. The boat zigzagged and maneuvered its way through the tight channel before docking near the edge of their property. I opened my eyes and was happy I had not fallen into the lake and the boat had not capsized.

We unloaded food, supplies and gear and carried them up to the cabin. The boat remained tied to the pier until our return to the parking lot at summer's end. The main room of the cabin was bright with daylight coming through the large picture window. Without electricity, we used gas lamps and candles. I watched the four children while the two couples spent time chatting and catching up with the latest. The women cooked over a wood burning stove while I fed the children and cleaned up by using water that was heated in a big pot on the stove. It seemed primitive, like the old covered wagon days of carrying water from the well and cooking with iron skillets, but for them it was fun getting away from life in the city. It was like camping out and enjoying nature, but better! Not to me, though; I didn't agree. At least we had electricity at home…

As dusk fell, out came the ice bucket, ice cubes, crackers, paté, celery sticks, olives and tall drinking glasses. Out came the laughter. The adults indulged in their nightly cocktails even when dinner was ready to be served, and I was treated to my own tall glasses of cold refreshing ginger ale or 7-Up, something I did not have at home. I quickly became addicted to the nightly bubbles as the laughter and conversations continued on and on.

The summer storms throughout Tahoe were common, dramatic and frightening. We watched dark clouds form and loom overhead as the skies turned devilish red, then jet black. With no curtains or coverings on the large picture windows, I witnessed dozens of lightning bolts touch down a short distance away, followed by tremendous, deafening thunder clashes, then torrential downpours. The whole house would turn pitch black as we dashed to light more lanterns and candles. The children squealed with delight or cried in hysteria, while my hand trembled so much it was hard to hang onto my "cocktail." I could not stop the ice cubes from clinking and dancing against the sides of my tumbler. If I was fearful, I did not show it and all the attention was turned toward calming the children first. I was happy at summer's end to be home and for me this was just another job, whether I liked it or not. The two couples treated me okay and did not show any concern as to how I felt or how I was doing. Mostly they were having fun.

I entered tenth grade in the spring of 1954 and turned fifteen in March. My low-tenth class increased in size from around fifty to nearly 200 with the transferring of students to Oakland High from the surrounding junior highs: Bret Harte on MacArthur and Coolidge, Roosevelt on Nineteenth Avenue (where Muriel had a year more to go) and a handful of students from Westlake. In contrast, the high-tenth class numbered 500-600 students. Every six months, each graduating class held its own ceremony in the school auditorium. One time Sammy Davis Jr. treated our student body and came to sing on-stage—little did I know how famous an entertainer he was.

I was elated to see the familiar faces of three of my friends from Westlake transfer to Oakland High: Bob Buckman, Lois Knickerbocker and Arlene Smith. In the meantime, Muriel seemed to settle nicely into Roosevelt, making her own new set of friends – lots of them Asians. I could hardly wait for her to transfer to Oakland High the next spring so that, hopefully, we would share the same lunch period and eat together.

Marilyn had graduated from Oakland High and was enrolled at Oakland City College. She quit working for the family in Piedmont and returned home to live. Now, at fifteen, I too was old enough to live and work away from home during the school months like Marilyn and Joanne had been doing. My first find was a family with kids in Oakland who owned an Italian restaurant in San Francisco. After school, I took the No. 59 or the No. 76 bus up Broadway Terrace past the lovely Claremont Country Club to the Upper Rockridge Area where the family lived. I did the most difficult work on Saturday—mopping, scrubbing, and waxing the floors on my hands and knees; in minutes, I was sweating and shaking. I moved every piece of furniture in the house to clean and dust behind each bed and chest of drawers, vacuum and then laundered all the sheets and weekly wash. At barely ninety pounds and totally out of breath, I wondered how long I could last doing this kind of work week after week. I lasted less than three months.

It was a blessing when Marilyn told me that Mrs. Krups, the daughter of her former boss, was looking to hire a live-in "mother's helper." I packed my things and waited dutifully again at the sidewalk for the driver. Mr. and Mrs. Krups picked me up and drove me to their home in Montclair, one block down the hill from Holy Names High School. Their residence was a one-story, ranch-style, three-bedroom house surrounded by tall trees in a woodsy setting, with a curved white picket fence lining the front yard to the garage driveway around the corner. Their two daughters, age three and one-and-a-half, had short straight brown hair and bangs that framed their cute little faces and dark brown eyes. Every day after school, I got off the bus at the top of the hill and walked down a long gravel country road alongside Holy Names High to "home."

When I first started cooking for them, I burned a few packages of frozen peas. I made all kinds of rice: brown, wild, pilaf, and Uncle Ben's, adding, of all things, gobs of butter. I did not know what converted rice meant, and I missed my plain Texas AA long grain rice as well as my favorite rice bowl, the white enamel one with the thin cobalt-blue trim. I learned to cook by following recipes in Irma Rombauer's "The Joy of Cooking," and it became my Bible in the kitchen, even for basics like cooking hard-boiled eggs. I learned to make poached eggs, Hollandaise sauce, rolled flank steak filled with bread dressing, tapioca pudding, and rhubarb pies. I made roast leg of lamb served with mint jelly and condiments of chutney, chopped hard-boiled eggs, raisins, chopped peanuts and shredded coconut. I cooked corn beef and cabbage and fresh artichokes. I made tossed green salads with tomatoes, radishes and avocados and literally drank Girard's French dressing straight from the triangle-shaped bottle because the flavor was absolutely delicious! With yellow onions, whole peppercorns, white vinegar and bay leaves, I made beef tongue in a pressure cooker that had a thing-a-ma-jig that jiggled on top of the lid when fully under vacuum, leaving the meat most tender. One time the cooker got so hot the lid cracked and flew across the kitchen, barely missing my head and denting the wall. When a new recipe which I tried to make turned out, I felt very proud. Remember, I was only fifteen at that time.

Each night I would set the dining table with a tablecloth and matching napkins placed in decorative napkin rings. When dinner was ready, I lit the candles in a pair of fancy candelabras on the table and announced, "Dinner is served." Serving Mr. and Mrs. Krups their nightly dinners was very formal and followed proper etiquette: taking dishes from the right side of the seated diner and placing dishes down on the left side. Some people really do live that way, like in the Shirley Temple movies!

Sometimes I carried a chunk of roast beef hot out of the oven on a heavy ornate silver platter for Mr. Krups to carve at the table. Making gravy from the pan drippings was a challenge; rarely was it smooth and lump-free, much to Mrs. Krups' chagrin when I handed her the gravy boat and ladle. I took my portion of food that Mr. Krups portioned out on my plate and went back to the kitchen to eat, at the same time listening for Mrs. Krups to ring her small dinner bell—my signal to dash through the swinging door with the next course. First was the salad, then the main entrée with a vegetable and starch, followed by dessert and coffee, which I brewed in an hour-glass-shaped Chemex carafe using large cone-shaped paper filters. By the time I finished serving the last course, the food on my plate usually turned cold. I then sat alone and ate slowly in silence before doing the dishes and cleaning up.

Mrs. Krups was a stay-at-home mom: tall, attractive with short dark brown hair. Young looking Mr. Krups was a quiet kind of guy. Since they had me as a live-in baby sitter and worker, they frequently went out on the weekends or invited company for dinner. When they were not home, I took the opportunity to play their 33-1/3 long-playing records on the Motorola hi-fi console, as well as my own 45 rpm extended-play records with the large one inch hole in the center, two songs on each side. I bought music by singers Joni James, Eydie Gorme, Tony Bennett, Nat King Cole, Glenn Miller, Tommy Dorsey, Les Elgart and George Shearing when their records went on sale from the regular price of $1.29 to 49 cents at Lucky's on East Eighteenth and Second Avenue. Regular 45's had only one song on each side, so the extended ones were a better buy.

One night while the Krups went out, I snacked on a whole can of smoked oysters in oil and spent the rest of the evening in the guest bathroom I shared down the hall. What a tummy ache, and I learned my lesson when one overindulges!

When friends of theirs came for dinner, I felt strange as I stood shyly before them and announced, "Dinner is served," like I was the maid. After dinner, they all progressed to the living room and played games, most popularly "3-D," a game like Tic-Tac-Toe but played on three see-through plastic tiers. They whooped and hollered and had a wild time… while I was trying to study in my room around the corner for upcoming exams.

I dreaded weekends when both girls, sweet and precious as they were, awoke at the crack of dawn and screamed to come out of the cribs in the room they shared. Pretending to be asleep and not hear them did not work for me for very long. Mrs. Krups came down from her bedroom to wake me up and then she went back to bed. No matter how tired I was and wanted to sleep in, what could I say? She was the boss. Little did Mom know how different I lived, and when I went home on my days off, she never asked.

Mrs. Krups' parents owned a rustic cabin at the Cedars in

Lake Tahoe, where two summers earlier I had worked for Mrs. Landers. Here in the summer of 1954, I was back at the Cedars, but this time with the Krups family. To enjoy the great outdoors and fresh air, our beds were pushed out on the deck and every night we slept outside. Our only sources of light were the moon and the twinkling stars that sparkled in the midnight sky. Oftentimes I could hear animals rummage through the garbage cans behind the cabin. Sometimes I heard the tiny, quick footsteps of squirrels and mice scurrying across the flat overhead canvas awnings, which were there to protect us in case it rained and to protect the cabin from the scorching heat of the day. One morning I found a dead rat on the deck floor next to my bed; it had fallen through a gap between the canvas strips. After that incident, I made sure I tucked in all the corners of my bedding and pulled one blanket edge well over my head, just in case an animal decided to fall on me.

Shortly after arriving at the Cedars, I met two young girls who were also working for vacationing families. Patty Ann was from Salinas, near Watsonville, two towns that are famous for their artichokes. Patty was tall with short, light brown hair. From a photograph she showed me, she and her brother had their own horses. He was fair-haired, blue-eyed and handsome, wearing a long-sleeved, plaid flannel shirt unbuttoned halfway, and tight denim pants that showed his thick, muscular thighs. The other girl, Patty's friend Susie, was blond, petite and full of spunk. Most baby sitters at the Cedars were given Thursdays off, so Mrs. Krups encouraged me to spend that time with my new friends. Patty, Susie and I talked, played Scrabble and went swimming. Because I did not know how to swim, they taught me to float in the pool using an old rubber tire. I thought it was wonderful for Mrs. Krups to give me the time off to be with my new friends, but on the other hand, I wondered why I did not have those days off when I was working for the Landers. Ummmm.

One Thursday night I stayed out so late visiting with Patty and Susie, I could barely see the landmarks along the dark, narrow dirt path leading back to my cabin. The bright moonlight magnified the shadows of trees as if they were ghosts dancing in the branches. I heard leaves rustling, imagining they were big, brown bears looking for a meal, or poisonous snakes preparing to strike. I was afraid that using my flashlight would give away my exact location, and every howl or little noise made my heart pound faster. I feared tripping over a fallen branch or a gnarly tree root, but finally I saw a light a short distance away. Mrs. Krups had left the light on to help me find the right lodge. Had I been any later, she would have sent a posse out to look for me. I know now she did worry about me, and she did care.

One beautiful crisp morning, Patty, Susie and I packed our lunches, brought fishing rods, and waded downstream where the creek met the river. Halfway across the width of the river were large boulders where we could stop to fish and have lunch. I took one look and said, "Hey, I can't cross the river. It's too deep, and I can't swim."

"Don't worry," Patty and Susie assured me, as they giggled and aimed straight toward the giant boulders. "It really is not that deep. No more than waist-high. Come on, be a good sport." I did not want to lose their friendship so I pressed on, even if it meant risking an early death. As I hastened to catch up to them, the water crept up to my waist, then my ribs, past my shoulders and neck, to just below my chin. The volume of water made me sway like a lone buoy in the middle of a lake and I felt my feet slipping on the rocks. I stretched my neck toward the sky like a giraffe, and held my arms high over my head to keep everything I carried from getting completely soaked. But I could do nothing about the Brownie camera that dangled from the long straps around my neck. Oh, no! I cannot afford to ruin my camera! I need it to take a couple of pictures of my new friends.

Finally I made it across to the gigantic boulders where Patty and Susie perched like a pair of proud eagles. I could barely see them through my water-specked eyeglasses. I emptied the water from my shoes and pulled off my clingy socks, then gobbled down my soggy sandwich as I cringed at the thought of going back the way we came. At that moment, I would have given anything to be back at my cabin, watching the colony of inch-long ants blaze their trails across the living room floor. Luckily, as I found out later, the photographs in my old camera did turn out, like the ones taken earlier of Patty and Susie floating atop car tires.

After that tour of duty, I spent the rest of that summer with the Krups at their other vacation residence in Alamo, a small town on the outskirts of Danville and Walnut Creek. It was about thirty-five miles east of Oakland, heading toward Mount Diablo in lovely Contra Costa County. The rolling hills were the color of wheat. What a contrast from the high mountains and lush green forests of Lake Tahoe! Driving on dirt and gravel roads, Mr. Krups brought us to the ranch. We passed signs that read "Private Property. Do Not Trespass," and "Cattle Crossing." Mr. Krups stopped and got out of the car, then unlocked a wide metal gate, swung it open and drove through, crossing a grate over an open trench. He stopped again to get out and close and lock the gate, explaining that the gates were there to keep livestock from crossing over or wandering off.

Mrs. Krups showed me to my room, a small shed next to the swimming pool, a few feet away from the main house. "Here are your sheets and bedding," said Mrs. Krups. "Tell me if you need more blankets. It gets very cold at night, even when it climbs well above 100 degrees during the day. When you are finished unpacking, come back to the main house, and we will start dinner." I stepped into the white wooden building and felt the musty dampness. The room was cool in comparison to the soaring temperatures outside. The floor was a concrete slab. A twin bed was at one side of the room by the door; a toilet and stall shower was at the other end. A couple of bathing suits and a pair of men's swimming trunks, faded from the sun, hung from hooks on the wall. The bathing suits had been there a while, along with old cobwebs and dead spiders. I decided to forego unpacking the things in my brown paper bag until later.

After dinner I used a flashlight to find my way back to what I labeled "The Outhouse." I changed into my nightwear and crawled into bed. During the night, the cold chill came through the walls, which were made from thin boards with no insulation. I awoke the next morning covered by layers of cobwebs that had been spun during the night by large black spiders that had come in to escape the cold. I battled my way like a wild child through a maze of webs, flaying both hands at arm's length to keep the stringy mess from touching my hair or tight lips. My stack of clothes and shoes across the room did not escape the spiders' artwork either. I wanted to go home. I asked for more blankets the next day.

Each afternoon when the girls went down for their naps, I took the time to recline on one of the chaise lounges by the pool. Borrowing and wearing one of Mrs. Krups' mustard gold-colored swimsuits, I stepped cautiously into the pool, but only if Mrs. Krups went in too, which was usually with the girls in the morning. The warmth of the sun felt good and I closed my eyes. I was on a beach in Hawaii watching the bright red sun fade slowly into the blue horizon, dreaming that one day a prince wearing silver armor would appear and sweep me off my feet. I dozed off, in spite of warnings about getting freckles and skin cancer later in life. Sometimes I awoke with an excruciating headache that stayed with me all night and into the following day.

Toward summer's end, I spotted bloodstains on my sheets. I would have panicked, thinking a rat bit me (as someone once told me about the bloodstains on her sheets), except at school a few months earlier, I saw a film during one of my Physical Education classes explaining a woman's menstrual cycles. Still, I was totally unprepared. I asked Mrs. Krups for help, and she gave me what I needed to use. Nothing else was said. I was afraid I would bleed right through my homemade gathered skirts and was relieved when "it" stopped… until it arrived again the next month, and the next.

When I returned home on my next day off and told Mom what happened, she said, "Oh, your thing came." She too had nothing else to say except, "You got so dark." That was the summer of 1951, and I vowed to look for another job… and once again stand at the curb with my personal belongings… with no goodbyes from Mom.

Mom, Susie Fong, standing far right in China in 1934 (age 24) with her three aunts; Front: her cousin, my great-aunt Goo Por, my great-grandfather Tai Goong, her cousin, my great-uncle (Goo Por's husband Mr. Shew), her uncle (Gnee Sook), and her cousin Bess.

My great-grandmother

Great-grandfather Lum Hung Sun in his 60s

My grandmother—far left

Mom and her sister

Mom, age 24

Mom, age 25, heading to U.S., 1935

My father Fong Man Dai

Mom in 1935

Great-Aunt Goo Por

Playground at Waverly Place, San Francicso

Joanne and Marilyn

Muriel and Frances at YMCA

San Francisco apartment rooftop

An outing in 1942

Lafayette Elementary School 1947—Frances seated far right, age 7, 2nd grade

1112 16th Street, Oakland, 1946

Living in one of the four units

Taking Vickie to DeFremery Park 1948

Mom with newborn Vickie, 1948

Frances wearing her new shoes and Joanne, 1950s

Marilyn, Muriel, Vickie and Frances in the 1950s

1528 Eighth Ave, Oakland, 1954 *Frances jumping the waves at Waikiki, 1956*

At Hana Maui Hotel 1956 *Babysitting boys near Diamond Head 1956*

Sigma Omicron Pi Sorority, University of California, Berkeley, 1958

Dressing up, 1957

Frances to Spring Informal, 1958

Frances UC Berkeley Grad, 1961

Stanley in the Army, 1957

Stan stood out like a sore thumb

Stanley and Frances wedding day, 1961

Son Brandon, age 8, Frances, age 33, daughter Bonnie, age 7, 1972

Susie Fong, age 68, 1978

Frances and Stanley, both age 50, 1989

Susie, age 95, Frances, age 66, in Brentwood, Ca, 2005

*Susie Fong (Frances' Mom), age 86
and Gladys Gim (Stan's Mom), age 84
at Rose of Sharon in Oakland, 1996*

Frances and Stanley, age 76, 2015

Frances, age 75, 2013

Frances and grandchildren,
(l-r) Amy, Nicole, David, Chloe, 2012

CHAPTER FOURTEEN:

PARTY DRESS

Upon my return to Oakland High in the fall of 1955, the secretary in the office said, "Here, take this address and phone number. The Vickers need a live-in to babysit their three children and help with the cooking on the weekends." Twenty dollars a month, including room and board, did not sound bad. So a couple of days later I went for a job interview. I boarded the No. 18 bus on Park Boulevard, got off at Excelsior Place and walked down the side of the Pacific Gas and Electric Sub Station along Grosvenor Place toward Trestle Glen. I made a right at Underhills Road. According to my hand-drawn map and directions, Underhills turned at the Oakland and Piedmont border into Indian Road, the street I needed.

The Vickers' beautiful two-story English Tudor residence was a couple of houses up the street, next to an empty lot. The stone driveway to the three-car garage was impressive. Mrs. Vickers, with shoulder-length, reddish-brown curly hair and brown eyes, reminded me of Bess Myerson, a television star and former Miss America. She gave me a quick tour of the house, showing me the wonderful oil paintings and life-size portraits she had painted. Period furniture upholstered in rich tapestry fabrics and a big, black, shiny grand piano were featured in the formal living room. French doors in the study opened out to a beautifully manicured garden and yard. After the interview, I headed home, relieved that I would not be spending the next summer in a cold, dark room full of spiders and webs. My move to Piedmont was to take place within a few days and once again, I was not sure how this family would treat me or if they would work me to death.

My room in the Vickers' house, one of the five bedrooms upstairs, was at one end of the hall and had wallpaper with tiny clusters of pink and red flowers. A window opened out like French doors where I had my own view of the lovely garden. The white bedroom set included a kidney-shaped vanity with a white, ruffled cotton skirt that swung open from a pair of wooden arms. Across the hall was a pink tiled bathroom that I called my own, with all the hot water I could want. Right next to my room was a door that was always locked; later I discovered this was Mrs. Vickers' art studio, where she kept her art supplies and easels and did all her painting. A tall bookcase right outside my door had a collection of books as well as stacks of programs on art and ballet. One night I sat on the floor in the hall and flipped through all the books with photographs of ballet dancers. The book featuring the Sadler Wells Ballet Company really intrigued me, as I wondered why I could not walk on my toes or point my feet the way the dancers did.

The Vickers were socialites. They either went out every weekend, attended parties, ballets, concerts and other cultural events, or threw parties and entertained at home. Mrs. Vickers would primp and dress up in elegant gowns and expensive jewelry. Often after partying the night before, she would sleep until it was time for her to get up and dress for another party that night! To keep the children quiet, I kept them in the downstairs maid's quarters, which was converted to a big playroom with lots of toys and a rocking horse. A wooden safety gate was latched at the door to keep their two-year-old Holly from wandering off. Conveniently, adjoining the playroom was a bathroom with a tub, where I bathed all three children before putting them to bed each night. Gray, named after his maternal grandfather, Gray Turner, was six years old. He was quiet and serious in nature like a typical first-born. In contrast, Keith, age four, could not sit still or stop talking, and Holly was adorable, with a mop of brown curly hair.

Putting Holly to sleep was a huge chore every night. She would not go to bed unless I crawled into her twin bed and read or sang her to sleep. She knew the minute I stirred and tried to sneak away. Sometimes it was 11 o'clock at night when I would finally awaken from dozing off and head down to the kitchen to clean up the dishes. I had yet to study and do homework.

When Mrs. Vickers planned for company, she would say, "Francie, let's make canapés today." She showed me how to remove the crusts (I thought it was very wasteful to throw away perfectly edible food) from each slice of bread, cut it into various shapes like hearts, diamonds and crescents and spread deviled eggs, canned deviled ham, liver paté or caviar, sprinkled with paprika and garnished with parsley on the bread. An hour later she would return and say, "Francie, let's polish the silver platters, serving pieces and candelabras. We need them for the hors d'oeuvres." After showing me an assortment of polishes, she disappeared again. It took me hours to polish and buff everything. I knew that every time she said "Let us," she did not really mean "us." Under my breath, I called her the "Lettuce Lady."

Mr. Vickers, on the other hand, reminded me of a young John Wayne, a kind and gentle person. He offered to drop me off at school on his way to work each morning. I watched him eat breakfast as he scanned the morning paper. After eating toast or a bowl of cereal, he fixed a tall glass of Tiger's Milk, adding wheat germ and molasses. I was always at the ready to follow him down the dark, narrow steps to the garage, where the strong smell of cat urine filled the air. I did not want to miss my ride, so I would hold my breath until the car pulled out of the garage.

After school I would take the No. 57 bus on MacArthur Boulevard and transfer to the No. 42 bus at Piedmont

Avenue. I felt uneasy when the kids from Piedmont High School boarded the bus at Highland Avenue and headed for the same neighborhood. As they laughed and talked noisily with each other, I knew they must have noticed I was not wearing a uniform like theirs. The girls wore white short-sleeved tops with starched sailor collars and navy blue pleated skirts. Each day I would arrive at the Vickers residence at 4 p.m., in time to take over for Ellen, the black full-time cook and daytime babysitter, who would start dinner before leaving her shift at 4:30. She had every weekend off. Then once a week, another black woman would come to do the cleaning. I would take over the evening duties and stay through each Saturday, preparing a full breakfast of bacon, eggs and pancakes or waffles. There I perfected making soft boiled eggs for the kids and poached eggs and Eggs Benedict for the others. Mr. Vickers would drive me home on Sunday mornings for my days off; I barely arrived home in time to rush off with Muriel to catch the bus to church in Chinatown.

One time when Mr. Vickers' car was in the shop for repairs, he made arrangements for the Turners' chauffeur to drive me to school. The driver showed up in his regular uniform, a black suit and cap, and a big black Cadillac. When he pulled his limousine in front of Oakland High, he insisted on walking over to the passenger side to open the door for me. I felt like Cinderella going to the ball… except I was not meeting a prince. I was glad when Mr. Vickers' car was fixed and he resumed driving me to school. It did not, however, stop the kids from eying me suspiciously from the corners of their eyes.

Then in late May of 1955, Mr. Vickers was sent to the Famous Dairy Plant in Honolulu, Hawaii, to handle some business for his father-in-law, Mr. Turner. Both men were executives in the company. Mr. Vickers planned to extend his business trip in Oahu by staying a few days in Maui, a neighboring island. Mrs. Vickers asked me, "Can you come along and watch the children? We have friends over there with children too, and you can go with us when we visit with them."

As far as I knew, Hawaii was a place only the rich could afford to visit. I did not know anyone who had ever gone there. It would be a treat to go someplace new, and they would pay my way. I nodded excitedly.

I needed approval from Mom and from my high school to make up the weeks of classwork in English, history, geometry, chemistry and third-year Spanish. Getting permission in writing from Mom was no problem. My sisters and I had learned for years how to forge her signature on our report cards and excuses as we duplicated the shaking of her hand while holding a pen to sign her name. My teachers were supportive. Some gave me assignments to work on, while others would test me upon my return. A few simply gave me their blessings. I worried about the upcoming Scholastic Aptitude Test (SAT), the one test I must do well on in order to get accepted into the University of California at Berkeley.

This time I borrowed a small light-blue color suitcase from Mom. The Vickers and I boarded a Pan American Strato-Clipper propeller airplane and headed to the island people called Paradise. What a spectacular bird's-eye view as we approached our landing! It was just like the pictures I had seen: blue water, white sand beaches, giant waves and lush, green, coconut palm trees swaying in the wind. Diamond Head stood out majestically on the point all by itself. The Royal Hawaiian Hotel, in all its pink grandeur, dwarfed the other buildings for miles.

We stayed in one of the thatched huts adjacent to the pool at the Edgewater Hotel. My bed was the sticky rattan sofa in the living room, with cushions covered in large floral prints. I had heard that thousands of termites love to gnaw at the damp window sills and wood furniture. In the late afternoon, the trade winds blew through the open windows and in the evening, hula dancers in grass skirts and Hawaiian musicians entertained guests sitting by the pool, surrounded by chaise lounges, round patio tables, umbrellas in an array of colors and rows of flaming torch lights.

While Mr. Vickers went to work during the day, the rest of us would go sightseeing or shopping, but mostly the kids wanted to go swimming at Waikiki Beach. I would walk knee-deep into the water and pretend I knew how to jump the waves. As the water ebbed, I could see the imprints of my feet on the warm, soft silky sand. If Mr. and Mrs. Vickers went out for the evening, our dinners were delivered by room service, so that was a real treat for me, not having to cook.

The beautiful Halekalani Hotel was a couple of blocks away from our hotel. When I had some free time, I wandered around the block and found a souvenir shop. I looked at a gold bracelet with dangling charms of hula dancers, palm trees, pineapples and ukuleles, but I could not afford to buy it. Instead, I bought a few postcards to keep as souvenirs and a colorful one to send home to Mom, hoping one of my sisters would read her my message.

A week later, we flew south in a small island-hopper to Maui and landed close to the rugged terrain of Hana Bay. The exclusive Hotel Hana Maui, accessible only by plane or four-wheel drive vehicle, rolled out the red carpet for us in the deluxe Kauwiki Cottage section, right on the golf course. I had a luxurious suite all to myself. The huge bathroom, with wall-to-wall mirrors reflecting multiple images, was bigger than my bedroom at the Vickers.

Right outside our rooms was a perfect view of the Pacific Ocean, and a few feet away were the pool and clubhouse where the hotel hosted Hawaiian luaus and staged entertainment. When Mrs. Vickers joined Mr. Vickers for a round of golf, she hit a hole-in-one. The hotel presented her with a small brass trophy in the shape of a number one with a hole through the center. When we returned to Piedmont, her trophy sat right on top of the television in the study, as a reminder of her achievement.

My classmates, many of whom were envious of my trip, were kids I had envied in earlier years when they would write essays on "What I Did This Summer," since I usually had nothing to write. One teacher was right, though… this experience could not be traded for a chapter in any textbook. And I did pass the SAT. So I had two reasons to be joyous.

One day Mrs. Vickers said, "Come, Francie. Let's go shopping. We are going to buy you a pretty black dress. You will need to wear it at Grandma Turner's big annual holiday party at her Glen Alpine Way residence. Lots of guests will be invited." I never had anyone buy me a party dress. Black would be fine; it is a classic color, chic, and sophisticated. I wondered what style Mrs. Vickers would pick for me. She dressed impeccably all the time, so I trusted her taste.

We arrived at the dress shop, a cute little neighborhood boutique like the one in Montclair or on Lakeshore Avenue. We searched the racks against the wall in the dressy dress section, looking for a black dress in size 5. The saleslady tried to find just the right choice for me. "How about this one?" she asked, as she held up a dress in front of me. I glanced in the mirror and my eyes lit up. It would make me look like a princess! Like Cinderella going to the ball! "Umm, no, not quite," replied Mrs. Vickers as she pondered, with one finger on her chin. She headed toward another rack across the room and thumbed through the hangers. "Maybe something not so frilly and fancy. Something plain and simple." Yes, I thought, it will not go out of style, and I can wear it again and again. Smart. She seemed to know what she was looking for.

"Ah, I think this one should do the job. Go try it on," said Mrs. Vickers. "It is perfect for serving food and receiving guests. Now we need to find a frilly white apron to complete the uniform." Immediately my smile turned into disappointment and hurt. The material was black faille—the dress was certainly plain and simple, buttoned down the front with a broad collar, lapel and pointed cuffs on the short sleeves. It looked like a housedress from the forties except for the full below-the-knee skirt cut on the bias, and it reminded me of what the waitresses on roller skates wore at Mel's Drive-In Diner. It fit me perfectly, but it was not a party dress. I tied on a white organza half-apron with a row of ruffles at the hem. I looked like a maid out of a Shirley

Temple movie.

As the guests arrived on the night of the party at the Turner estate in Piedmont, I stood next to the butler and greeted each one at the door. I asked, with a bit of a curtsy, "May I take your coat?" Then I took each guest's wrap, purse or hat to a designated room. Mrs. Turner's regular staff of servants scurried about, while extra help was hired to work in the kitchen. I served trays of hors d'oeuvres to the guests circulating on the first floor, returned used and empty cocktail glasses to the kitchen, and emptied ashtrays, which left a residue on my fingers and a lingering smell I could not wash away for days. As the guests left at the end of the evening, I retrieved their fur coats and mink jackets. By the end of the evening my feet hurt, I was hot and sweaty, and my crisp new dress was wrinkled.

This was no way to enjoy a party. I wondered if I would end up living the rest of my life like Ellen or the cleaning lady, doing domestic work. I thought back to the times I was cooking, washing dishes, babysitting and changing diapers, or on my hands and knees scrubbing floors. I thought, not if I can help it. I was beginning to understand why Mom encouraged my sisters and me to study hard. It was time for me to do even better in school. It was time for me to look for another job–a better job. When I left the Vickers a few months later, after working there a year, I did not take the pretty black dress. It stayed, wrinkled, on a hanger in my closet. Aloha.

CHAPTER FIFTEEN:

MIGHTY HIGH

In January of 1956, my senior year of high school, I was tired of taking care of children and needed to find a different kind of work so that I would have more time to study. I worried about doing well enough to be accepted into college. Again, the best I could find was a live-in job with the Walkers, a family who lived in a beautiful white house on Woodland Way in Piedmont, near where upper Mandana Boulevard becomes Crocker Avenue. The work, however, was the same as I had been doing—cooking and cleaning—but at least there were no babies to take care of in this family. Living away from home would also continue to help Mom with keeping her expenses down.

Mr. Walker worked in an office at the Kaiser Company in downtown Oakland. Mrs. Walker, tall and slender with short light-brown hair and a demure smile, had facial features, elegance, and mannerisms resembling the actress Julie Andrews, the star of the movie, "The Sound of Music." They had three children. Crissy was blond and fourteen years old; Scott had light brown hair, was thin and lanky, and twelve years old; and Penny was the red-haired nine-year-old. Each child had a pet dog. Mopey, a small white dog that yapped a lot, belonged to Crissy, and Scott and Penny had Mike and Patty, two large brown dogs. I was sixteen, happy to find a home with three older children and doubly happy when Mrs.

Walker offered to pay me more than what I had earned at the Vickers.

The Walkers' home was a white, two-story wood building. Upstairs were four bedrooms and three bathrooms: a master bath, a private bathroom for Crissy and a bathroom that Scott and Penny shared, nestled between their separate bedrooms. A beautiful wooden staircase from the entry hall led to the upstairs hall, where a hidden laundry chute went straight from upstairs to the first floor below. I thought whoever designed that was ingenious.

A tall, square-shaped glass jar filled with an assortment of imported, individually wrapped Pascal hard candy sat on top of the large desk in the entry hall. The candy caught my eye and made my mouth water. My eyes zeroed in on the yellow ones, the sour ones. I bet the lime-green ones were sour too. A large ceramic cookie jar in the kitchen was usually filled with thin chocolate wafers that quickly became my favorite cookies. I grinned when Mrs. Walker said, "Please help yourself anytime to the snacks." I quickly realized that as soon as her children arrived home after school each day, the cookie jar emptied out (with my help!). Sometimes the ever-famous black-and-white chocolate Oreos were substituted for the wafers.

The family gathered for all their meals at the formal dining table, set with cloth napkins that were neatly folded and placed into decorative napkin rings. Every morning Mrs. Walker placed a small, clear plastic packet of colorful capsules and tablets at each place setting, making sure every family member took their daily dosage of vitamins. I did not get any.

I sat and ate my meals at the long formica counter in the kitchen, next to a large window that overlooked a lovely backyard garden. My room with a private bath was the servant's quarters, located past the kitchen through a large pantry and storage room. At mealtime, all three dogs would thunder down from the upstairs through a secret set of back stairs to the pantry, to their dishes of food and water. They scared me. What a sound as all three ate from their dishes in unison! Slurp. Slurp. Slurp.

In the living room was a grand piano, which I longed to play. The only time I played a musical instrument was when I was loaned a violin under a music program to introduce music to fourth-grade students. I cried when the year was up and I had to hand my violin over to another student. As I was preparing dinner, I could hear Crissy practicing on the piano. I would peek into the living room and listen to her play. When no one was home, I took her sheet music for "Deep Purple" out of the piano bench and practiced playing by memorizing the placement of my fingers for every note in the entire piece. It was truly music to my ears! When I heard someone coming home, I quickly tossed the sheet music back into the bench, made a beeline back into the kitchen, and rolled my eyes—relieved that I had not been caught.

Crissy was keen and smart, with an outgoing personality. When she spoke, she smiled a lot and her eyes sparkled. She seemed so grown-up for her age. She decorated her room with a collection of fans above her headboard, and her bathroom vanity had an array of makeup, cosmetics and perfume atomizers. Other than the times I was dusting or vacuuming around the house, I would sneak into her room and marvel at all the pretty things she had: matching bedroom furniture, a bedspread with ruffles along the edges, feminine baby doll pajamas, a pair of fluffy comfortable slippers, and especially, the pretty things in her bathroom. I never got caught looking. And I never took anything, although the temptation was there. After school, I starched and ironed the sailor collars on Crissy's middy tops for her to wear to Piedmont High, a very prestigious school. As I was just two years older than she, I hoped Crissy and I would become friends.

When I received my paycheck after the first month of work, I frowned at the amount. It was less than what I had expected. When I confronted Mrs. Walker that perhaps a mistake had been made, she explained she was complying with the employment laws and had to deduct a percentage of the gross pay for payroll taxes, so my net pay was smaller. What a bummer! I had never heard of such a thing! Taxes. That year I earned $483 of which $9 was withheld for Social Security, an amount I was to receive back someday when I was old and retired. But I would rather take the much-needed pay today. I will never get old. But what could I say? She was the boss. Besides, working for the Walkers was not bad, considering I could eat all the cookies and candies I wanted.

Every night when I retired to my room, I would play my own "Name that Tune" game, or listen to music or baseball—the Oakland Oaks and the San Francisco Seals—on the radio while cramming in homework and studies.

That summer, two adults, three children, three dogs and I piled into the Walkers' big station wagon and headed to the coastal town of Balboa, just south of Newport Beach and Costa Mesa, and north of Corona Del Mar. Nearby was Laguna Beach, a popular artists' colony. The dogs paced back and forth and jumped impatiently between the front and back seats during the day-long drive to Southern California. I sat in the back row of seats and became nauseous from the dogs' odors, their tails constantly wagging in my face.

The Walkers' brown shingle ocean-front summer home was on the corner of Ocean and Seventh Street. One could see the Pacific Ocean through the large front windows, and the view was even more spectacular from the second-floor master bedroom picture window that also faced the ocean, just a few feet away. There is something very special and calming about watching the soft rippling of the ebbing waters and the whitecaps of the ocean waves.

The children's grandparents had a home a few blocks away. Their backyard was a private beach that faced Newport Harbor on the bay side, and every day the kids and I walked to Grandma's house for a swim in the inner harbor, where they tried to teach me to swim. "Come on, Frances, jump in! You will float with no problem," they said, running to the end of their long, private wooden pier and jumping in feet-first while pinching their noses with one hand. I could not swim like they could. Instead, I waded out until the water came up to my shoulders, turned 180 degrees, and paddled and kicked, face down, back toward the shallow end, standing up only when my hands touched the sandy bottom. Although I did not ever like water on my face, I did succeed in learning to float on my back. Still, I hated whenever water went up my nose, making me choke and sputter like a whale. They were right; I could float more easily in salt water than in a swimming pool.

One afternoon, as I was swimming back toward the shallow end, my head fully submerged in water and holding my breath for dear life, I felt someone's hand grasp one of my arms just below the armpit. It was Mrs. Walker, yanking me by the arm until I was upright. "And so, young lady," she muttered, "just where do you think you are going?" I was startled when my feet could not touch the bottom. Apparently I had made a wrong turn and headed toward the deeper waters of the harbor beyond the pier. If Mrs. Walker had not seen the situation and jumped in after me, I surely would not be here telling this story. I still have nightmares about that incident—images of gasping for air and trying to reach the surface of the water several feet above my head.

The children each had their own small sailboats. Every year they entered into the annual summer boat races called, I believe, Flight of the Snowbirds. The big challenge was to find a friend to be the "crew" or assistant on their two-person team. Unfortunately, I did not watch them race or know the outcome, but I heard there were lots of entries in this event. One time a group of kids from a big family around the corner came with us to an annual carnival several blocks away. I was awed by the huge crowds and bright lights. And I remember, while walking back late that evening, feeling proud and happy to be accepted as a member of their group. That was the only time I did anything socially that summer.

When I came home at the end of the summer, Mom did not realize how lucky she was to be able to say to me, "You are so dark!" This time, I was happy to be dark… and alive. I was also happy to return to school, to my last semester of high school before graduation.

Mr. Art Olsen, my high school counselor, called me into his office one day; this was a rare occurrence. He spoke softly, with a big smile that showed his high chipmunk-like cheeks and his upper teeth, and he wore a bow tie. He was gentle and kind—the fatherly type that perhaps I wished my Dad could have been. "Well, Frances," said Mr. Olsen, "I know you wanted to make it into the highest 10 percent of your spring class of 180 students. You placed twentieth, so unfortunately you just missed. However, you made Seal Bearer, the highest academic honor based on the total number of semesters you were a member of the California Scholastic Federation, and that is quite an achievement. More importantly, you were accepted to Cal. Congratulations!"

Mr. Olsen also told me I had won the Bank of America Achievement Award in the category of Home Economics. More than likely, my Home Econ teacher of four years, Mrs. Pearl Welsh, nominated me. She was petite and wore her dark hair pulled back neatly in a chignon, the look of a ballerina. If I thought Mrs. Welsh was fussy about hand-basting each seam, she was even fussier when it came to machine-stitching. She checked and measured the width of every seam and the proper length of each stitch before we could proceed to the next step of our project. Although I loved sewing and made my own clothes, I decided I was never going to sew for a living. It did not seem like a good career. Besides, Mom told me sewing gave her gas and made her stomach grow.

Mrs. Welsh was one of my favorite teachers, partly because of the subject she taught. Another teacher I highly admired was my ninth-grade homeroom teacher, John Hills. He was young, freckled, and blond, with a crew cut and an infectious smile. Out of all the students in my class, he chose me to write a famous person's quote on the blackboard, because I had the best penmanship. Every day our class discussed his selection, and then we wrote the quote in our notebooks. He went beyond the call of duty as a homeroom teacher to give us a taste of literature. I will never forget him, or his good looks. I think I had what one would call a crush on this teacher!

When ninth-grade students from other junior highs like Bret Harte, Roosevelt and Westlake transferred into the tenth grade at OHS, I was shifted from Mr. Hill's class to Dr. Ross' homeroom. She taught Spanish, but my own favorite Spanish teacher for nearly four years was Mrs. Vittorini Brush. She was tough and strict, and she made a big impression on me, like Mrs. Welsh did, as well as Wilbert Yuen in biology, Karl Cooperrider in English, and Mrs. Neal in P.E. at Westlake.

Miss Louise Jorgensen, who conducted the annual Christmas Pageant for the Oakland Parks and Recreation Department when I was at Westlake, thrilled me when she appeared years later at Oakland High and selected me along with a group of other students to dance in the "Hours" number one year and again in the "Light of the World" the following year. Leaving Westlake did not mean my chances of being in the pageant were over! Mrs. Jorgensen choreographed and redirected these dances for many generations, and she was an Oakland icon. As in all the previous years, the production ended with her in the same role in the finale as the "Spirit of Christmas" dressed in flowing chiffon while hundreds of tiny little fairies in short white dresses skipped across the auditorium floor to surround her. One year she was injured and could not dance, but the spotlight was still on her as she appeared in the finale in a wheelchair. She retired in 1987 after directing 62 shows. Sadly, she passed away in 1995. An article in the November 23, 2006, *Oakland Tribune*, stated there was an attempt to revive the Christmas Pageant in Oakland as a Winter Festival, but that was short-lived. No one else could replace her.

Since I continued to dance in the Christmas Pageant at Oakland High, I was no longer sad or angry that I was kicked out of Westlake.

When I was between jobs and lived at home, Muriel and I

would catch the No. 18 bus to school. One year there was a bus strike and we had no choice but to walk to school and back. We took the most direct route, up Eighth Avenue, down Ivy Drive and over to Park Boulevard. Every morning we passed our schoolmate Virginia Chan's house. Her father was outside hosing off his car before taking his daughters to school. When he offered us a ride, we jumped at the opportunity. After that, we had a ride every morning as long as we were on time, and he meant On Time! Sometimes we ran our legs off so that we wouldn't miss our ride; when we were early, we sat on the sofa in the living room and waited. While Virginia and her two younger sisters, Irene and Vivian, finished their breakfast and readied for school, Muriel and I listened to the classical music playing on their hi-fi system. Before Virginia turned off the turntable and put the long-playing record back into its sleeve, she carefully wiped the dust off with a soft cloth. Obviously, she was taught to be responsible and respectful of their belongings.

My greatest fear in high school came when the brand-new Live Oak Swimming Pool was built right next to Oakland High on MacArthur Boulevard. In order to graduate, every student was required to take swimming during gym period and pass a swimming test. I hated getting into the pool, even though it was heated. I hated putting on a swimsuit and taking a shower in front of other girls, and putting on a lovely white rubber swim cap with small colorful flower petals; it did not help to keep my hair dry.

"Put your face in the water," hollered the woman instructor, who had very big arm muscles. "Blow bubbles. Arch your back. Put both arms straight in front of you, and kick like hell!" I did all that in the shallow end in three-foot-deep water, but I could never float. It was as if each foot was held down with lead. All I could feel was water seeping through my swim cap. I clung to the edge of the pool and hoped the teacher would not notice me, until her booming voice roared out, "You, the one with the flower petals flapping in the wind. Go out to the middle of the pool and swim back toward me." She really did not need a megaphone as she repeated, "Put your face in the water, blow bubbles, arch your back, both arms in front and kick like hell!" I did, but without my eyeglasses, which I left in my gym locker, I could not see where I was going. Everything was blurry, no matter how hard I squinted, and I knew I reached the side of the pool only when my hand touched it as I frantically gasped for air. The period was over, and I was saved by the bell.

The lessons went on, but I never learned to swim. I was relieved when it was announced that our class was waived from the swimming requirement because we had not been given enough time to learn to swim. In hindsight, perhaps I should have been forced to learn; I still cannot swim!

I did not have much of a social life in high school because immediately after school, I was on the bus to my job as a "mother's helper." In the tenth grade, I ate lunch on the school lawn with my friends Edith and Jeanne until I got a job cashiering in the teachers' lunchroom and was compensated with a free lunch from the teachers' menu. I dated no one, did not attend school dances and went to one after-school football game, with my sister Muriel. It was exciting to hear the roar of the crowd and participate in the school yells. That was when I decided to run against the school jock Bernard Butler as yell leader for our class. Why not? I watched the school cheerleaders and booster girls waving their pom-poms and told myself, "I could do that!" Well, it was just as well that I did not win. My voice would never carry. Afterwards, I felt like a fool.

Absolutely my best memory of high school was taking Driver's Education, a class that taught students how to drive a car. The class that followed was Driver's Training, where a student with a learner's permit actually learned how to drive on the nearby city streets. I took a Saturday class with two other students in the car and a driving instructor, Mr. Wetmore, who sat on the passenger side with his own set of brakes, which he did not hesitate to use in case we were going to crash. Two students sat in the back seat while one student did the driving; the positions rotated so each student had a turn to drive. The car was a stick shift, rather than an automatic; the trick in shifting gears was to raise the clutch pedal slowly with the left foot while accelerating the gas pedal just enough to make a smooth transition or the car would sputter and lunge, or worst yet, you would kill the engine.

In those days, cars did not have turn indicators. To signal a turn or lane change, we stuck our left arm out of the rolled-down front window on the driver's side, rain or shine: arm straight out meant a left turn, arm up meant a right turn, and arm down next to the car door meant a stop. I remember Mr. Wetmore emphasizing the two most important rules of driving: 1) steering – a must, in order to have full control of the car at all times, and 2) passenger comfort. The true test was how safely and smoothly we drove the stick shift without jerking the passengers around. Too bad my Driver's Ed classes ended after a few weeks.

When it came time for the senior ball, I talked for weeks in my Spanish IV class with my friend Gail about how badly we wanted to go. We were just dreaming. I wanted to wear a real party dress and feel like Cinderella, even if the clock struck twelve and I had to be home by a certain time. But who would ask me for a date when I was such a dork? I wanted to be asked by this Chinese student body officer, but he was not paying any attention to me, even though he knew I was one of the smartest girls in class. I kept my hopes up but instead, I was asked at the last-minute by a boy I did not want to go with. I decided if I could not go with the one I wanted, I would not go at all, so I declined what could have been my first date. And I could have collected my first "bid" from the dance as a souvenir and be the envy of the girls who did not go!

All the "could haves" and "should haves" meant I wasn't so smart after all… I was so determined to go only with the "popular" boy that I ended up not going at all. Was I stubborn, or stupid, like that white student body officer who wrote in my yearbook, "You might be smarter than me in

English—but how come I get better grades than you do?" then wished me "Lots of luck in the coming years." Now if he really was smart, he would know the answer to his own question, wouldn't he?

At the end of high school, several teachers signed my yearbook and stated I was the best cashier in the teachers' lunchroom. I was accurate and speedy and always ready with the correct change before the teachers even approached the cash register with their trays. One jokingly wrote I owed him a discount because he ate exactly the same thing every day and I did not have to add up the dishes on his tray! By working in the teachers' cafeteria, I learned each teacher's idiosyncrasies, quirks, personalities and spending habits. I even knew which ones were the tight-wads! One male teacher who took a very long time to dig down into his small, worn-out leather coin purse for the exact change was the worst. He, not I, held up the line.

Soon I will no longer be a "high and mighty" senior. I will miss my classes and teachers, especially the tough ones like Mrs. Welch and Mrs. Brush. I will miss eating in the cafeteria with Muriel and her friends. Along with the fun I had participating one semester working on the Oaken Bucket Yearbook staff, I also had fun in the clubs I belonged to: Chi-U, High Power (a Christian group), Delegate Assembly, and Acorn Council. These are my high school memories.

As I walked down the long, slanted aisle of the school auditorium on Graduation Day past the rows of tiered seats and stepped on-stage to receive my diploma from Principal Paul Pinckney, Mr. Olsen's words rang in my head: "Good luck at Cal. Good luck at Cal," and I quickly realized I would need more than luck to make it through college. Mom did not come to see me graduate.

Mr. Olsen's daughter, Zoe Ann Olsen, was an Olympic diving champion in 1948 and 1952. She married Jackie Jensen, who played for the New York Yankees and Washington Senators. Other notable graduates from Oakland High were Ralph Edwards from the television program,

"This is Your Life," Chris Burford, a Hall of Famer who played for the Kansas City Chiefs; and Edwin Meese, United States Attorney General from 1985-1988.

Go, Oakland High!

WHITE MAN'S WORLD

One by one we left you
My three sisters and I
Did you ever wonder?
Did you wonder why?

We entered into the white man's world
Had a roof over our heads
Felt the warmth of their cozy homes
Slept in their comfortable beds

High up in the hills, Mom
Fancy mansions were their homes
Each one had several bathrooms
I even got one of my own

There were China dishes
Pots of Revere Ware
Crystal vases, serving platters
Flatware of polished silver

Some homes had grand pianos
With shiny keys black and white
And Hi-Fi with stacks of records
I played them night after night

They taught me to cook from recipes
Using "Joy of Cooking"
No matter how hard I tried and tried
The frozen peas kept burning

I learned to use a blender
Mastered the pressure cooker
Ate artichokes and leg of lamb
And ice cream straight from the freezer

Now I cook with wooden spoons
Spatulas made of rubber
But really take my word for it
Chopsticks work much better

I did their dishes not by hand
But placed them in a washer
Flipped a switch, then let them dry
I guess that was a lot cleaner

I did the wash and ironed their clothes
Starched each shirt and dress
Bathed their kids and put them to bed
Then went to my room to rest

Turn the knob on my radio
Listened to each song
"Name that Tune" as each one played
Try not to get any wrong

Time to hit the books now
There's no more time to waste
I am tired and my eyes are blurry
Trying to get straight A's

As I turn my radio off'
I am happy to be alive
I tell myself take one day at a time
I simply have to survive

Finally I turn my lamp light out
Thinking of things I miss
I pray to God I would not have to live
The rest of my life like this

CHAPTER SIXTEEN:

OLD TIME RELIGION

Back in my grammar school days at Lafayette School, my sisters and I had the option of attending a "religious instruction" class at the denomination of our choice. With Mom's permission to leave our classes an hour early once a week, we chose the Volunteers of America because it was a short walk from school. We earned gold stars for naming the Old and New Testaments and extra stars for memorizing and reciting scriptures from the Bible. We snacked, made crafts and sang songs like "Jesus Loves Me," "Jesus Loves the Little Children," and "The Old Rugged Cross."

Since Mom was a devout Christian, she also sent us to Sunday school there, which reinforced her teachings for us to behave like good little girls. I remember the time one of the teachers said, "You cannot go to heaven unless you believe in God. Do you believe in God?" I raised my hand and nodded for fear of going to hell. I kept my head down and my eyes closed.

After moving to Eighth Avenue, Muriel and I attended Sunday school and Summer Vacation Bible School next door at the Elim Tabernacle Church, which was very convenient. Later, the church was sold to a black Southern Baptist group and Muriel and I stopped going there. We used to stand on our chrome dinette chairs and peek from our kitchen window through the stained glass-and-frosted windows of the church to see what was going on. When the sermons and gospel choir got heated, we watched silhouettes of the congregation sing, clap, stomp and shout "Alleluia," "Praise the Lord," and "Amen" as they marched up and down the aisles. The organist banged even harder on the keys. At times the singing became loud and boisterous, to the point that the members sounded hysterical. We had to close our kitchen windows to cut down on the intrusive noise, but usually to no avail. I was scared from the emotional outbursts and frenzy, and I imagined that the church members often fainted. Alleluia.

About the time Muriel entered Oakland High in 1956, we knew several classmates who went to the Chinese Presbyterian Church in Oakland Chinatown, on Eighth Street between Alice and Harrison, so we decided to join them. As soon as I arrived home on my day off, Sundays, Muriel and I rushed to take the bus to Sunday school.

Mom recalls that during this period, Muriel lived and worked for a couple in Piedmont but after a few months, when she expressed unhappiness with one of her bosses, Mom told her to move back home. By this time things were better financially at home; Muriel could help shop for food in Chinatown, keep a watchful eye on Vickie and start dinner while Mom was at work.

Much, much later I found out that Muriel had a very unpleasant experience with the man of the house where she had lived and worked. This is what Muriel remembers and relayed to me by e-mail in October 2004. "I don't even know how I first started the job, whether Joanne and Mommy asked me to work there or whether I asked for the job. It was when Joanne graduated from high school, so I must have been 14 or 15. All I remember is I took the #42 bus on Piedmont Avenue to Piedmont with other domestic servants, all of them black. Upon arriving, my first task was to get past the family pet, a big golden retriever who greeted me by jumping on me. She could have knocked me down because she was so big! I was told to step on her paws, which is what

I did [in order to get her to stop]." *(Imagine how terrified I would be had I been in her place!)*

"After putting my things away in my very small room in the kitchen area that had a bed and a table in it, I went into the kitchen to see if the Mrs. left me any notes. If not, I would look for her to ask what had to be done. I didn't have any routine things because someone else did the heavier cleaning and washing before I got there. My job as a mother's helper was basically to prepare and/or cook food for dinner, using recipes or instructions the Mrs. left for me. Usually she was not home when I arrived; I think she was out playing bridge. I don't know and I didn't ask. I learned to follow recipes and use ingredients I never encountered before at home, for example, making rhubarb desserts."

"Around 5, she came home and shortly after that, the Mr. arrived home from work. After they finished their cocktails, I served dinner in the dining room. They liked to barbeque frequently; the Mr. did the grilling. When they were through with dinner, I ate in the kitchen by myself, washed the dishes and went to my room to do my homework before cleaning up for bed. I don't remember it as being hard work–in fact, I remember walking around their house a lot, just looking at things. I thought their house was so pretty, and I loved being in Piedmont."

"The couple (in their 60s) was never unpleasant or harsh with me. But I only worked one semester. The reason was, every day when the husband, who was very tall and seemed very old to me, came home, if his wife was not around, he came into the kitchen, walked right up to me and kissed me on the lips! I tried pushing him away, but he was a lot stronger than I. I never said anything to the Mrs. or anyone else, but I knew I didn't like it and I knew I had to get out of there."

"I'm not sure what I told Mommy or Joanne, but I did not take another mother's helper job after that. Luckily at that time, I was studying office practices in high school, including shorthand, and was good enough that my shorthand teacher referred me to a job after school at Grayson's, a women's clothing store downtown."

I suppose there are many untold stories like Muriel's that happened to other mother's helpers. It angers me that abuses and atrocities like that went on and never got reported to the authorities because we did not know what to do nor were we resourceful. Did these things happen to Marilyn or Joanne? I don't know. Luckily, nothing like that happened to me in all the jobs I had; perhaps God was looking out for me, like he looked out for Mom.

Early one Sunday morning, our Sunday school teacher, Walton Robert Lee (Bob), spotted Muriel and me waiting at the corner bus stop on Foothill Boulevard. He pulled over and kindly offered us a ride, and from that day on he drove us to church every Sunday. I thought Bob was the most handsome, youthful-looking Chinese man I had ever seen. He was very articulate, had a wonderful speaking voice and a warm smile. I am sure I was not the only girl who had a crush on him. Plus, I saved on my bus fares!

For lack of church space, our youth group met upstairs in the balcony overlooking the sanctuary. I took my classes seriously, completing every lesson in my workbook. He motivated our class by encouraging participation in oral discussions where we would argue and debate our different views. Bob was a wonderful educator. From him I realized that things were not always either black or white, and that there were many shades of gray. Two people who disagree with each other can both be right. Even about religion.

Bob was also the playground director at Lincoln Square in Chinatown. Many times I tagged along with Joanne to the weekend dances at that clubhouse. I sat there with my hands crossed on my lap and waited for someone to ask me to dance. Once in a while, I looked up in time to see a guy stroll right in front of me, hesitate and then continue walking around the room, looking for a better girl. Oh, how I hated that! No one ever stopped to ask me for a dance. Perhaps next time...but there was no next time… week after week.

While Muriel and I chose to attend the Presbyterian Church, Joanne went to the Chinese Independent Baptist Church on Webster, next to a gas station on the corner of Ninth Street. She knew many of the kids there and made lots of friends. A few years later, that church built a new building on Eighth Street, between Harrison and Alice, across from the Chinese Presbyterian Church. Further down on Eighth was the Chinese Methodist Church and a few blocks away were the Episcopal Church of Our Savior and the Japanese Buddhist Church.

My youth group at church was very important to me: outgoing Crystal came from the neighboring town of Alameda; pretty Alice came from Berkeley; and Bertha and Elena were two of many who came from the Ming Quong Orphanage Home on Ninth Street in Oakland. A large contingency of girls from Oakland included Judy and her cousins Cynthia and Carole, Virginia, Brenda, Priscilla, Darlene, Kitty, Charmaine, Rose, Jeri, Carolyn and her sister Camilla. Some of the guys were Tommy, Ricky, handsome Peter, jovial Stan and his brother Steve. It was a neat bunch of kids!

One time Crystal, Tommy and I sang as a trio in front of the whole congregation. I was scared and my knees were knocking the whole time, but I was proud I went through my first time ever performing in front of an audience. I had no idea, however, how well I sang. We had some wonderful choir teachers. First, there was Steve Lee; his wife, Anna, played the organ and his daughter, Carol, played the piano. Next was Ed Fung, then George Jung, who was totally blind and walked with a cane. Bob Lee's wife, Lonnie, often sang solo during church services. What a devoted and talented group of people! Eventually Muriel and I joined the choir. After the rehearsals following the church services (at times we met on Friday nights) on Sundays, a group of us would walk to a local restaurant. I checked my coins to make sure I had enough money or else I could not join them. For forty cents, I had a bowl of won ton soup at the New Chung King

Restaurant on the corner of Webster and Tenth Streets. It was owned by my friend Shirley Yee's family. If I had enough money, I also headed by bus to the Broadway Bowl on Twentieth Street near Telegraph for a round of bowling with the youth group.

When church announced a snow trip to Donner Pass near Lake Tahoe for the youth group, I wanted to go badly. But I could not afford to sign up until I was offered a scholarship to help defray most of the costs. It was the first time I had experienced snow. Without the proper waterproof ski attire, though, the tiny snow flurries melted through my clothing, especially the red plaid wool scarf I had wrapped across my face to protect against the chill. As I brushed the droplets away, they soaked through my knitted gloves, making my hands colder than ever. Brrrr! I was disappointed how quickly the snowflakes melted in the palms of my hands and turned into water. For some reason, I thought real snowflakes would be the same size as the 6-inch snowflakes I cut out of construction paper and displayed on the windows and walls at school.

As I started college, I drifted away from attending church during the school term. However, for the next few summers, I did resume going to church and sang in various church choirs. I suppose that was still mainly for social reasons, and that was a very important time for me, of learning to grow up…

CHAPTER SEVENTEEN:

SIGMA OMICRON PI

At age seventeen, with IBM punch cards in hand, I registered in the spring of 1957 at the University of California (Cal), Berkeley. Robert Gordon Sproul was the President of the University System at the time, followed by Clark Kerr in 1958; Dr. Glenn T. Seaborg was the Chancellor at the Berkeley campus. Tuition was $25 a semester. After enduring registration lines that snaked along for blocks, I ran from building to building across campus to pre-enroll for my classes. If a class was full, I would show up on the first day of school, hoping the professor would add me to the roster or allow me to replace a student who had dropped out. Amazing that this is all done by computer now.

Buildings on the Berkeley campus stretched from the Greek Theater and the International House on the east side to Home Economics and the School of Public Health on the west. Bancroft Avenue and Sather Gate were at the south end of campus. Hearst and Euclid Avenues bordered the North Side. At the center of campus was the landmark Campanile, a replica of the one in St. Mark's Square in Venice. The elevator to the top of the bell tower provided students and visitors with an amazing view of the entire San Francisco Bay Area.

My sister Joanne was in her second year at Cal, majoring in Public Health. As a member of the Chinese sorority, Sigma Omicron Pi (founded in 1930 at San Francisco State College and formed on the Berkeley campus in 1947), she introduced me to her sorority sisters. I wanted to experience what sorority life was all about, so I pledged, along with Janet Chinn, Jennie Hong, Donna Tom, Valerie Ng and Stella Shao in February at the Black Sheep Restaurant, where a complete steak dinner cost a mere dollar. Janet from Oakland, Jennie from Mill Valley, and I went through all the steps to become the newest members: rushing on February 15 at an informal tea held at Stephens Union, pledging, hazing and the final initiation. It seemed there was a social event once a month: a joint dinner-dance with the Chinese fraternity Pi Alpha Phi at the Pioneer Village Restaurant, a Big-Little Sister potluck dinner, fund raisers and a skit for a dance rally. There was the Spring Informal Dance at the Surf Club in San Francisco and a Winter Ball in December held in the Golden Empire Room at the Mark Hopkins Hotel in San Francisco. We were a classy and busy bunch! At the end of the semester, I was voted the Outstanding Pledge.

The Chinese fraternity Pi Alpha Phi (members were known to us sisters as the Pineapple Pies) had a resident house on Warring Street. The International Fraternity Council had recently ranked this group top in overall grade point average. Its new pledges were Dennis Tom, Ted Tom and Francis Lum. Joanne was dating one of the frat members, Dennis Chin from Berkeley, a microbiology major. As far as I knew, he spent a lot of time at the Life Sciences Building doing research in the lab with rats and guinea pigs. When the frat held house parties, Joanne was naturally Dennis' date, and they did not seem to mind that I tagged along. I noticed many of my sorority sisters paired up with the fraternity guys. Eventually many of the couples ended up marrying, but I was not one of the chosen girls.

Six months later, a new group of pledges joined our sorority. Mimi, Claribel, Marsha and Sylvia came from the same high school in San Francisco and were always together. Carolyn, who lived on Upper Mandana Boulevard and was my best paddleball partner in high school, and Edith, both from Oakland High School, were the other two pledges.

The sorority participated in Chinese club activities with other campuses too, such as in 1960, at the annual three-day conference with the Chinese Students' Intercollegiate Organization. Contestants for the "Sweetheart Queen" came from San Francisco State, U.C. Medical Center, City College of San Francisco, Sacramento City College, San Jose State, USC, UCLA, UC Berkeley and other colleges. Stunning Maeley Lock from my hometown represented San Francisco State. Fu-Yi Ching was the beautiful candidate representing Cal. Toni, as we called her, called me Mama Frances because of the preponderance of motherly advice I gave her, and she came out the winner. For the Annual Spring Informal Dance sponsored by the Chinese Students' Club, Joanne fixed me up with a blind date from the fraternity. I bought a beautiful white dress on sale at I. Magnin; it had soft scallops and a light-blue ribbon across the bodice, and long streamers down the front. The ballerina-length net billowed over a full satin skirt. The dress was several sizes too large, but I altered it down to a size 7. It matched perfectly with a pair of white satin open-toed sling heels. I had a good time that night.

But after a year of activities that I was ill-equipped to handle socially, academically, or financially, I gave up my sorority membership. Dropping out was a relief, as I looked forward to spring 1958, when Muriel would be joining Joanne and me at Cal. Imagine, the three of us would be at the University of California and none of us relied on, or even knew about, the process of applying for scholarships or student loans although we were in such dire financial straits. Muriel was dating Ricky from church; he was now a civil engineering major at Cal, Joanne was seriously dating Dennis, but I was still without a boyfriend, money or good grades. I had no business being in the sorority; I had no business being at Cal.

One time it angered me when I heard that a fellow student had run short of money and just called home for more. A hefty check, I think around $1000, arrived for her in the mail shortly after that. Not fair!

CHAPTER EIGHTEEN:
UPS AND DOWNS

In the summer following graduation from high school, and just before I started Cal, I was seeking a higher-paying job to help with my college expenses. I had already left my live-in jobs before I graduated from Oakland High. I found out just how hard it was to find work in a store or office. However, I had heard that I. Magnin, a 5-story high-fashion store on Broadway and Twentieth, hired only young Chinese women to run its elevators, which meant I stood a good chance of being selected. Sure enough, I landed a job working weekends and holidays, the only openings available. I. Magnin was a beautiful store in the heart of downtown Oakland that sold very expensive items.

My trainer took me down to the dark and dingy basement. Machinery sounding like a generator rumbled in the background. On one side was the shipping department. Exclusive, two-toned light-and-dark-tan striped gift boxes filled the shelves in another section. On the other side, chain-link fencing formed storage cages, each one securely locked to safeguard racks of designer dresses and pallets of merchandise. Toward the back was space where I could change into my uniform. For privacy, I dressed behind a row of lockers and then ran up the back stairs to punch my time card. The standard uniform was a black tailored suit jacket fitted at the waist, a short straight skirt and a pair of white gloves.

On the main floor by the two front entrances, floral fragrances, spicy colognes and woodsy musk oils from the cosmetics department permeated the air, causing me to sneeze and my nose to run. Nearby was a bank of three elevators. Elevator No.1 was the newer automatic elevator that went to the fifth (top) floor, where Alterations and the Employees' Lunchroom were located. There was a round, swing-away seat for the operator. Ruby Gin, the full-time operator who scheduled our shifts, and a few senior operators ran this much-to-be-sought-after elevator.

Elevators No.2 and 3 with the wider doors ran manually, by flipping a lever attached to a large circular dial on the wall. Steering the lever with my left hand to the right or left made the elevator go up or down; releasing the lever set the brakes. Without a safety gate or door, we literally saw a wall of doors with black floor numbers flash in front of our eyes as we ascended or descended. My right hand held a thin wooden baton to keep customers back; the same hand flung open the heavy doors. All day long I repeated "Floor, please," and then announced "Mezzanine: Cashier's Office and Ladies' Lounge; Second Floor: Fine Apparel and Furs; Third Floor: Dresses and Lingerie; and Fourth Floor: Children, Gifts and Beauty Salon." I was happy when I was allowed to relieve the operator of preferred Elevator No. 1 for her breaks, because I was able to sit down. By the end of the day, my white gloves were soiled from touching levers and door handles.

Elevator No. 3 was mainly used for employees or freight. We did, however, also use it to transport an overflow of customers when there was a special event, like a fashion show or trunk sale. Sale days were pandemonium, with hordes of crazed shoppers, particularly during the holidays. Sometimes my elevator landed too high or too low. I gave up after several attempts and told customers to watch their step as they exited. However, if I did not like the customer, I intentionally left the elevator too high or too low, hoping he or she would trip. Thankfully, that never happened, or I would have been sued or out of a job!

After four months of working part-time, I was lucky to be retained full-time that summer, because business would pick up during the summer months. I even helped gift wrap in the shipping department, where I ran into my second cousin, Bess, who was working there. Mom recently revealed to me that when Bess, her first cousin, got married to Clayton Soohoo. Dad attended the wedding and banquet, but Mom did not go, because in those days it was not popular for women to go out to parties in public–only the men did. So Mom missed her first cousin's wedding. But remember, Mom went dancing and partied when she first arrived in the United States.

I loved handling the fine merchandise in the gift department of I. Magnin, touching the smooth, pretty taffeta gowns, soft angora sweaters, silky baby-doll pajamas and thick fluffy towels with monograms. There was even an "I. Magnin secret" of how the flat knot of the ribbon was tied on the gift boxes. Once I worked overtime and took inventory after store hours, counting bras on the first floor. Imagine sorting them by various sizes and hand-tallying them on sheets of paper a painfully slow process. After all, there were no UPC bar codes then. I earned over $800 that summer, but it was not enough for the entire year of college, especially keeping up with the sorority activities. It was never enough money, even after I quit the sorority. Hard as it was to work the elevators, I had fun running them with Ruby, Ellen, Margaret and Jackie. My hope was to have this job again next summer because it was the best work I could find with that kind of pay and not having to live or babysit in someone's home.

The following summer, in 1958, I lost the elevator job but found a sales position at Tai Ping Company in San Francisco Chinatown, on the corner of Grant Avenue and Sacramento Street. The store sold porcelain and Celadon green vases, colorful cloisonné, carved red cinnabar boxes, brocade blouses and Oriental dolls. It also carried lacquer ware, grass mats, rattan furniture, Japanese prints, Dong Kingman watercolors, jewelry and an array of souvenirs. Customers interested in rosewood and teakwood furniture were directed to the mezzanine floor, where the more experienced salespeople presented their spiel. The main attraction was a tall, intricate, silver replica of a pagoda that nearly reached the ceiling, on display in the middle of the store. Inside a glass display case were two other eye-catchers: a long, hand-carved ivory tusk (which is now illegal to import), as well as a set of graduated hand-carved ivory balls, the largest about 6" in diameter, magically set snugly one inside another, with no openings or seams.

The store's owners, Tom and Amy Hong, lived conveniently above the store on the third floor with their three school-age children, Merrily, Dexter and Candace. An elevator behind the cashier's counter took them up to the front door of their custom-built apartment. Petite, sophisticated and demure, Mrs. Hong wore custom-fitted *Cheong Sam* dresses and was the store's cashier. Mr. Mon Wong, thin, lanky, wearing black-rimmed glasses and a suit and tie like an accountant, was the store manager. What a character he was as he dashed around taking care of business in his very business-like manner! What made me laugh was when he would make faces, twitching and using his nose to raise his eyeglasses.

The three older salesladies, Ruth, Grace and Emma, were the loyal permanent employees; they had the early shift, from 9 a.m. until 6 p.m. Doris Lee, a vivacious high school student from Reedley near Fresno (she was staying in San Francisco for the summer), the Hong's oldest daughter Merrily, her classmate Maelene Leong and I made up the rest of the work force, working the special summer hours from 1:00 to 10:00 p.m., which was the closing time for the tourist trade. Each of us on the sales staff wore cotton coolie jackets with mandarin collars and frog buttons, alternating each week between red and light green colors. Doris and I would end up as best friends by the end of summer, but more on her later.

Mr. Hong, tall and proud, assigned each of us a section of the store to dust and keep the shelves neatly stocked on display. Mr. Hong eyed every move we made. "Displaying three of each item is a good number. Any more than that confuses the customers and they cannot make a quick decision. They tend to walk away and not come back to buy, even if they say they will," said Mr. Hong as he dashed around and moved merchandise throughout the store with an artistic flair. I was intrigued every time a salesman dropped in to make a sales pitch with Mr. Hong. What did they talk about? What kinds of deals were being made? I wanted to know, but I didn't know how to ask.

One time Mr. Hong teamed us up (young with old, but omitting Merrily) to see which pair made the most sales in a certain period of time. As an incentive, a small cash reward was offered at the end of the contest. I enjoyed selling and talking to the customers; many of them came back to buy from me. I thought I had made the most sales each week, but my partner did not do so well, so we lost the prize to another team. Although the amount was small, I could have used the bonus money.

At closing time, I would run up the back stairs behind the cash register, peel off my coolie uniform, grab my jacket and rush off to the San Francisco Transbay Terminal at First and Main streets. I would hurry through the dark, deserted Financial District with haunting shadows of skyscrapers towering over me, pass Montgomery Street and cross Market Street while listening for footsteps that could be from someone who might do me harm. As I arrived at the terminal nearly out of breath, I ran past the derelicts who were asleep on the long, slippery, wooden pew-shaped benches and up to the second level. If luck was with me, I could catch the early bus. If not, I got home to Oakland around midnight.

One Saturday, a Cal classmate, Diana Wing, invited me to a house party in San Francisco. I made arrangements to stay overnight with my friend Ruby, who had moved from Oakland to San Francisco for her elevator job at I. Magnin. I borrowed her light blue, embossed brocade dress and pulled my hair back sophisticatedly into a French twist. I looked pretty good! At the party I met Steve, nine years older than I, a graduate in electronics from Cal Poly Tech. Steve spoke my Cantonese *Heung San* dialect. That would please Mom. As a young boy, he had lived in the Nanking Building, the same one on Sacramento Street where I was born. Also, by coincidence, my mom knew his mom.

Steve, a very good dancer, and I went dancing at The Log Cabin on the old Bayshore Boulevard in South San Francisco, where a street sign on the highway said "Entering San Mateo County." A gorgeous Chinese female singer sang her sultry rendition of "My Funny Valentine," accompanied by a Chinese trio led by a handsome musician on keyboard. On other weekends, we would dance at the Chinese American Citizens Alliance and the private Square and Circle Club. We attended the Miss Chinatown Contest at the Masonic Temple and went to the Coronation Ball that followed a week later at The Fairmont Hotel. We went sunning all day in our swimwear at the nearby towns of Fairfax and Larkspur in Marin County, sometimes changing and staying to dance outdoors under the twinkling stars. We dined downtown at the famous Lefty O'Doul's Restaurant and frequented Miz Brown's and Hippo's on Van Ness, famous for their deluxe hamburgers, as well as Mel's Drive-in Restaurant near Fisherman's Wharf, where waitresses on roller skates brought our order on trays to our car. Steve drove me to places in San Francisco I had never been to before (places he labeled "Inspiration Points") like Coit Tower and the Marina, where we saw beautiful views of the thick fog rolling through the Golden Gate Bridge at dusk, where he put his arms around me and said tender words, and where he stole kisses until sunrise.

The match seemed ideal, but Steve was very critical. One time we passed a dress shop on our way back to his car. He pointed to a matronly-looking dress on a mannequin and remarked, "Now, that's the kind of dress you should wear."

That puzzled me, but I was not going to confront him about it. My best guess was that he did not like my homemade clothes. When he proudly showed me the clean engine under the hood of his 1956 Chevy, all I could muster up was, "It's cute." He gave me one of his dumb "Charlie Brown" looks and mumbled, "Rats," while he rolled his eyes again. Steve was also a radio ham. He tried to teach me Morse code, but I had difficulty with the correct number of dots and dashes (or dits and dahs), that represented long and short elements of the letters of the alphabet, numerals, punctuations and special characters. I can see him rolling his eyes again. At least I learned his call letters, K6EOW.

I dated other guys too. Steve's friend Dan was pitifully shy and not a good dancer, but at least he took me dancing. There was that guy all the way from Redwood City, somewhere down on the Peninsula near the Circle Star Theater in San Carlos. And there was that sweet-talking, soft-spoken, Hawaiian boy Randy from City College. Like his buddies, he was obsessed with kissing his date an entire evening in a dark corner. Then there was the one I met when I went to the Chinese Baptist Church for a short time. He brought me home to meet his mother; I could tell immediately from glancing at the heavy, black teakwood furniture in their living room that they were well-to-do. One night he picked me up at my home in Oakland and took me to Lake Merritt. He rented a small paddle boat and we pedaled around the lake for about an hour. When it turned chilly, he offered me his jacket and seemed like a gentleman, but I never dated him again. I guess he either did not like where or how I lived or did not want to know me better.

Doris Lee, one of my co-workers at Tai Ping, and I became good friends. Doris had beautiful skin, a bright smile and lovely almond-shaped eyes. We talked for hours as if we had known each other for years, a no-no at work, as Mr. and Mrs. Hong eyed us to get back to our separate stations. I cried about not having a real boyfriend I could call mine. "Chalk it all up as experience," was Doris' advice, "even the bad ones. Most of all, keep your chin up." She was very talkative, but she did not divulge much about her life or why she was living in San Francisco for the summer. She mentioned having a step- or half-brother in Hanford, near her hometown Reedley. I promised that in the fall I would take a Greyhound bus to visit her. As she was a couple of years younger than I, she seemed mature for her years—so confident and sure of herself. So pretty too.

Doris and I double-dated with Steve and his band of buddies: Dan, Jerry, Paul and John. Doris, attractive and intelligent, ended up running for Miss Chinatown. Steve and I continued to date steadily for the next few weeks. At work, I kept my eyes on the clock toward closing time, my heart thumping and palpitating, happy to see him show up with his pleasant smile and deep laugh lines. I was a serious young lady on the outside and a little giddy girl who did not know how to behave on the inside. He was coming to take me out; I had witnesses in the store who saw him. I was very happy, but as summer came to an end, so mysteriously did our dating. Disappointed again, I could not claim he was my boyfriend.

CHAPTER NINETEEN:

WILD CHILD

For the next two summers, I returned to work at Tai Ping on Grant Avenue, although I would have preferred a different job with better pay. But I did not know where to look for one. I guess there was a good enough reason to return to Tai Ping for the third summer in a row: Mom tells me Tai Ping means *Ping On*, and that means between the earth and sky, there is no war or crime, just peace.

In my third summer at Tai Ping (1960), I convinced the Hongs to hire Brenda Choye and Nancy Lee, Muriel's classmates at Oakland High School, even though neither of them had the work experience I had. They commuted by bus from Oakland for the late evening shift, but, unlike me, who commuted alone, they had each other for company. This time I was assigned the normal day shift hours from nine to six; I was lucky when my friend Ruby Gin asked me to share her apartment, just one block away from Tai Ping. With her transfer to the I. Magnin store in Downtown San Francisco, Ruby moved into the new three-story Salvation Army Residence for Women on Waverly Place and Sacramento Street, which replaced the former Salvation Army Center. I was so happy, because I saved commute money as well as time, and also, splitting the rent and sharing the food expenses with Ruby helped her financially. Ruby's small studio apartment on the second floor had two twin beds, one nightstand, a tiny kitchen space and a small closet stuffed with pretty dresses and shoes. The two windows in her unit looked down onto the traffic of Waverly Place, and the view was the front of the Chinese Baptist Church, where I had gone to Chinese School in the first grade.

Ruby was a beautiful young lady: thin and trim, she wore her jet-black hair short and wavy behind her ears. Her face, as well as her nose, was long and narrow which made her all the more beautiful, and she had lovely thick eyebrows that accentuated her long eyelashes. She did not have the typical look of an Asian. She was very thoughtful, often having dinner ready for me when I came home from work, and she did not always charge me for my share of the grocery bill. When she did a load of laundry, she would check to see if I had any clothes to add to the wash. When I went out on dates, she often loaned me her store-bought dresses, many of which she bought at a discount as an employee at I. Magnin. And if I ran short of money, she would loan me enough to tide me over until my next paycheck.

Ruby's recipe for Fiesta Tamale Pie Casserole was my favorite. In a large pot or frying pan, sauté one small yellow onion (chopped) and one clove minced garlic (I use 1 tsp. of prepared chopped garlic) in 3 tsp. butter and 3 tsp. olive oil, until onion is limp. Push to one side, add and brown 1 lb. ground beef or turkey and ½ lb. pork sausage in same pan, breaking and stirring meat (do not drain). Add one large can diced tomatoes (3-1/2 C), one can corn, not drained (2-1/2 C), 2 tsp. salt and 1 tsp. ground chili powder. Simmer 20 minutes and pour into 9 x 12 baking pan. Press and stir 1 cup yellow corn meal, 1 cup milk, 1 can pitted olives (drained) and 2 well-beaten eggs into mixture. Sprinkle 1 cup grated mild cheddar cheese on top. Bake one hour in 350 degree oven, or until mixture bubbles at the edges. This serves 15. So yummy!

On the weekends Ruby kept busy with her boyfriend, John, a pharmacy student at the University of California San

Francisco Medical Center. One Saturday he gave us a tour of the lab, pointing out specimens of diseased parts of the human body preserved in jars of formaldehyde. One very swollen part on display was infected with Elephant's Foot Disease. I shivered as I peered at the various displays, and I could smell the odor of ether and chemicals permeating the air. I wanted to gag. On the other hand, I was glad I took the opportunity to take the tour when John offered because many of my classmates at Cal, after taking pre-med classes in Berkeley, transferred there. To name a few, there was cousin Ellen Louie, who went into Physical Therapy; friend Clifford Lew, who majored in Pharmacy; and many of the boys from the Chinese fraternity. I started out in Dental Hygiene, but switched majors due to low grades in Chemistry, especially Organic Chem 8.

No longer commuting home every night, I took an active role in my social life. I didn't need a date to go by myself to the weekly Friday night dances at the YWCA, and I could dance with different partners. During this period, I resumed going to church. I attended the Cumberland Presbyterian Church and joined the weekly choir practice sessions. In the choir those who befriended me were Alan, Stacey, Walter, Milton, Michael and Louise. Church became a big part of my social life again. After services, about eight of us went out for won ton soup and chow mein noodles. Often I was the only female in the group and became the center of attention, because perhaps I was young and naïve. I was teased and easily flattered by the guys. Most were at least ten years older than I, out of college, working full-time, single, and, I suppose, looking for love or someone to marry. Dr. Pon was a dentist. Marrying a doctor would be nice, I thought. Milton, an engineer with the California Department of Transportation, was thirty-two, with a receding hairline. He was still living with his parents out in the Avenues and soon became my compassionate friend, sometimes, much to my delight, paying for my share of the tab: forty-five cents for a bowl of won ton, the cheapest item I could order off the menu, just in case I had to pay for my own lunch. He was gentle, soft-spoken and quite convincing when he shared his viewpoints, which intimidated me, since I had not yet formed my opinions.

When Milton shared his season tickets with me to Arthur Fiedler's Summer Boston Pops Concerts at the Civic Center, I thought I had hit the big time. We sat in the balcony and watched elite patrons seated at small round tables with red-and-white-checked tablecloths. It was quite a sight to watch the candles flickering on top of each table as the theater lights dimmed. Once Mr. Fiedler took the stage, raised his baton and the program started, everything settled to a hush. All we heard were the orchestra, the clink of glasses and an occasional wine bottle rolling across the main floor. We went to see Shakespeare's "Much Ado about Nothing" and "Bells of Campobello," a play about President Franklin Roosevelt, portrayed by an actor in a wheelchair. Milton took me to the San Francisco Ballet, which I knew nothing about, except for seeing pictures of ballerinas in books and programs. Every time the audience clapped, it was my cue to clap too. Some whistled wildly. Others shouted, "Bravo!" It seemed strange to witness such outbursts from an audience that I assumed would be reserved, but after attending a couple of performances, I realized it was the acceptable thing to do as a show of appreciation for the performances. At the end of some of the concerts, the finale would be followed by applause and shouts of "Encore, Encore" until the curtains opened and the audience settled into a hush once again when the orchestra performed an extra selection.

My challenging and exhaustive late-night talks with Milton were mostly on philosophical subjects, from "everything happens for a reason" to "either do something about it or forget it"—like lessons in life… taught by him… to me. And he also grilled me on what I thought the moral of the play or movie was that we had just seen. I wondered if my answers were what he wanted to hear. He told me I was magnanimous, a word I ran home to look up. Did he really mean I was "noble of heart and mind"? Anyway, it pleased me that he thought that highly of me.

At summer's end, I moved back to Oakland, thankful that Ruby shared her apartment with me. With Joanne married in 1958 and now living with Dennis in an apartment close to campus, I no longer slept on the green sofa in the living room but in one of the three beds in the dining room that I shared with Marilyn and Muriel. Now I had the use of Joanne's old chest of drawers, the one with curved sides and the decals of cute animals in the center of each drawer. Night after night, just like at the end of the last two summers, I sat by the telephone, waiting for it to ring. Men I had dated all summer long seemed to forget I existed. *Was I a novelty? Was I that naïve? Maybe I was not pretty enough. Maybe living across the Bay was not convenient.* I sobbed quietly under my blankets so as to not disturb Marilyn, asleep in her bed next to mine, and Muriel asleep in the divan across the room by the swinging door into the kitchen. I finally fell asleep with my face buried in my cold, wet pillowcase… wondering what had gone wrong. But that was not all that happened to me during the summer of 1960.

I usually left Saturday nights open to attend the young adult dances at the YWCA on Clay above Stockton, across from Commodore Stockton, which was my first grammar school. I walked unescorted to the Y, puffing up several steep blocks in heels to meet up with friends from church. The dance room was dark and noisy. Men outnumbered women, so a line of men waited their turn to dance. I did not sit out a single dance. It did not matter that my feet hurt from wearing cheap shoes, or that I got blisters from the narrow pointed toes. No matter how tired I was after standing all day at work, I had to dance. It was worth all the pain and suffering.

If someone did not offer me a ride home by the end of the evening, I hobbled home alone around midnight, avoiding dark alleys, elated that I got in another night of dancing. Clopping downhill in high heels was no easy task, not in San Francisco! But nothing got in my way of dancing—not even fear of the dangers of night. In college, I would choose to go dancing rather than staying home to study, even if I knew the odds were I would flunk an exam because dancing was my priority.

Each week at the Y, I spotted the best dancers in the dance hall. That was where I met Joe, the married man. Joe was a smooth dancer… the best. He was slender and handsome, with youthful looks and a flat-top crew cut. There was an air of mystery about him as he and his shadow paced and darted around the crowded room looking for a dance partner. He spoke softly with a distinct Chinese accent—perhaps a recent immigrant. We danced, and as our foreheads touched, his beads of perspiration were apparent. We felt each others' sweat through our clothes. Even our arms stuck to each other like flypaper. We danced close and moved like one body. We kept time to each tune—first a tango, then a fast swing, a hot rumba and finally a romantic fox trot. For a few minutes, the packed dance floor cleared and a ray of light through a crack in the ceiling beamed down on us. With a strong lead, he whirled and twirled me in perfect timing around the room. We danced to the tempo of an elegant waltz—slow… quick, quick; slow… quick, quick. For a few seconds I, Ginger Rogers, was in the arms of Fred Astaire. It was far better than dancing with a partner when I took ballroom dancing in Physical Education at Cal.

When Joe first asked me out, it seemed harmless. A few dates later, I questioned him about how he could go out night after night without his wife. His answer was that she was happy staying home with their baby as long as he was happy going out with other women. Yet it never occurred to me that what I was doing might be hurting her. Here in the back seat of Joe's car, parked in front of Ruby's apartment at three in the morning, he was on top of me, pinning my hands against the seat. His hands started to reach inside my skirt. At first I thought I could sweet-talk him out of it, but then I was scared that in a split-second he would violently attack me. Physically, I knew I was no match for him.

What was I thinking? What was I doing with this married man in the back seat of his car? These thoughts raced through my mind as we continued to kiss. He stopped, reached into his pocket and pulled out something small and rubbery… something I had never seen before. I had heard about men using such "things" for protection. I had read books and seen enough movies to realize he wanted something more from me that night than just making out. Did the idea of dating a married man intrigue me? I heard my heart thump loudly, and I was sure he could hear it too. Mom had warned my sisters and me for years about *Hom Sup Lo,* dirty old men. She did that from the time she sent us alone to the Chinese movie theater when we were kids in San Francisco and warned us not to talk to strangers. When she heard rumors about a friend's daughter dating someone non-Chinese, running away with men who had wives and children in China, eloping or getting pregnant while single, she lectured us to stay away from bad men. And she would repeat, "People will talk." If I had a bad dream that someone was chasing me, I could escape by bounding down flights of stairs in a single leap and wake up in a dazed stupor and cold sweat, my bad dream broken...but this was not a dream.

How could I end this nightmare? Mom's words of warning echoed and faded in and out of my ears: "*dirty old men… people will talk.*" I dared not bring shame like that to her. I repeatedly told myself not to do it, although I did not know what "doing it" was, or how it was done. I pleaded with Joe to stop. He got up slowly, zipped up his trousers, hesitated and let me out of the car. Then he sped away.

My hands trembled as I tried to find the keyhole to unlock the glass front door to Ruby's apartment building. I stumbled up two flights of stairs. I had done a very foolish thing. That same morning, I prayed to God for forgiveness and to keep me a virgin, whatever that meant.

CHAPTER TWENTY:

THE BLACK CLOUD

One summer day while I was working in San Francisco, Mom was scheduled for either her gallstones or one of her kidneys to be removed (this was the period in her life when she had so many health problems). I arranged to take the bus after work to meet my sisters at Herrick Hospital in Berkeley. Stopping at the information desk to ask for Mrs. Fong's room number, I was directed to the Intensive Care Unit. The floor nurse in charge was emphatic. "Your visit is no more than five minutes in I.C.U. I'll come back when your time is up," and she disappeared quickly as she pointed to Mom's room. I did not know what to expect as I pushed on the heavy swinging door and tiptoed into her room.

Mom was hooked up to all kinds of machinery, and she was in a coma. I think the nurse was trying to tell me my Mom was dying. The first things that caught my eye as I approached her bed were dots of light flashing and blinking on the equipment board next to her. Several plastic tubes protruded from her nose, mouth and arms. Her eyes were shut and her pale face had swelled to twice its normal size. Her curly hair stood on end and its slightly gray hair color had now turned white. I did not recognize her. I surmised that whatever medication was given to her had made her whole body bloated, and the surgery must have shocked her system. Poor Mom!

I leaned over her bed rails and stretched toward her face, so close I could have kissed her cheeks. Then I spoke Chinese to her in almost a whisper. "Mommie, this is *Som Mui* (third daughter). Do you hear me? Where is everyone? Did they not come today to see you?"

Couldn't she at least blink her eyes and acknowledge my presence? I inched closer to her face and asked again in a louder voice, "Where is Marilyn? She said she would meet me here with the rest of them," but Mom did not respond with any hint of movement. Being so close to her face frightened me because our family never got that close to hug or kiss. The only time I came that close to Mom was when she used to scrub my face with a washcloth when I was a child—then I could smell the fresh fragrance of Pond's Cold Cream on her face. My time was up. The nurse nudged me through the swinging door, assuring me everything possible was being done to make Mom comfortable; I left with the impression that Mom had only minutes to live.

It was dark outside as I boarded the bus on Telegraph Avenue. I was confused, upset and in tears as I stared out the window. Mom was dying, and I did not know where my sisters were. I groped for my house keys as I got off the bus and headed toward home. As I entered the hall, all four of my sisters jumped up from the green sofa in the living room.

"Where were you?" they chimed together. "We waited, but we assumed you were working late or were stuck in traffic. Mom is doing fine. She asked about you."

"What do you mean, where was I? I saw Mom at the hospital, dying! I thought she had just minutes to live. She could not say a word to me."

I suddenly realized that the Mrs. Fong I visited at the hospital must not have been my mother. Since I did not specify Susie Fong to the receptionist, I was given the room number to the wrong Mrs. Fong! No wonder I did not recognize her. I felt bad, then shocked, then stupid. What a fool! I hoped the other Mrs. Fong did not hear the things I had said to her. What if she did not have any daughters? What if she had one, but did not call her *Som Mui*? I hoped I had not sent that Mrs. Fong to her grave faster. I cringed at the thought.

In all those years since Mom arrived in America, she has not spoken English. Interpreting, and helping Mom take care of business fell on Marilyn's shoulders at a very early age, until it was her younger sisters' turn to help. One time I accompanied Mom to the Ear, Nose and Throat Specialist, Dr. John Metheny, when she kept coughing and complaining of having severe sore throats. With a tongue depressor, Dr. Metheny looked into her mouth and saw small white bumps on her throat. She gagged. "Mrs. Fong, you have a bad infection in your throat," said Dr. Metheny. "I will prescribe medication that will clear it up. Today I will scrape and medicate the sores to speed up the healing. It will sting a little. When this condition clears up, I recommend you have your tonsils removed, since you persistently get these sore throats."

I watched Mom wince, choke and gag again. Suddenly a dark cloud came over me, as if someone had poured a bottle of black India ink on top of my head and it was leaking through the cracks of my skull. It dripped down my forehead and covered my eyes. My legs wobbled and gave way, like Jello made with too much water. My head hit the wall, knocking down the floor lamp with a loud crash. Minutes later I opened my eyes and saw Dr. Metheny using smelling salts to revive me. I was of little use to my Mom the rest of the day as she accompanied me home on the bus. After that, Mom knew better than to have me help with her medical appointments. I was better dealing with numbers and financial matters, like bookkeeping, writing checks and paying bills. Even sewing, knitting and doing macramé beat going to the doctor with Mom.

Soon after Mom's throat healed, she took Dr. Metheny's advice and had her tonsils removed. This time my sisters said to me, "Go on your own after work to visit Mom." The hospital hall smelled sickeningly of ether. Mom was the only patient occupying a bed in the multiple-bed ward. She was asleep, heavily sedated, and groggy. She did not hear me, and I did not want to awaken her. Just then she turned to one side and coughed to clear her throat. I ran over, grabbed a pan and placed it under her chin as she gagged and spit up blood. The last thing I remember was Mom reaching for the bell to ring for the nurse. I awoke to find myself recuperating on one of the empty beds next to hers. Once again, my mother, the patient, was tending to me, the visitor. How bizarre!

One day a few years later, I received a frantic telephone call from my mother. Uncle Donald, my dad's younger brother, who used to take us on outings to Golden Gate Park and the De Young Museum, had fallen on a sidewalk in Oakland Chinatown. She could not reach anyone else. She needed me to help him at Highland Hospital—the same hospital that gave me my first pair of eyeglasses in grade school. When I arrived, he was lying on a gurney in the hallway by the emergency entrance, waiting his turn to be examined. An ambulance roared up to the entrance with sirens wailing, dropping off an injured victim. The attendants whizzed him past us to the emergency room for immediate attention. Finally one of the doctors was free to examine my uncle. Mom stayed in the lobby to wait while I went to interpret for Uncle Donald in one of the small examination rooms.

"How did you fall? Does this hurt?" the doctor asked as he pressed against my uncle's stomach, then his ribs.

"Ow, yes. It hurts."

"I'm sorry. I'll try not to hurt you, but I need to find out if you have any broken bones or serious injuries."

The doctor lifted my uncle's hospital gown. Both legs were swollen. The areas were terribly infected. He could not walk without great pain. No wonder he fell.

"How long have you had this? It looks horrible. Does it hurt here?"

"Ow, yes. Please don't press so hard, doctor."

It pained me to see my uncle suffering. Here comes that ebony black cloud again. My legs wobbled again like Jello and in minutes, I felt faint. I remember seeing the doctor wave frantically for an aide to bring a wheelchair for me. I sat in it, with my head slumped to my chest, as the aide wheeled me out to the lobby. I saw my mother look up; it did not surprise her. She knew she should not have called on me to help in a medical situation.

I hoped the doctors took care of my uncle and that he arrived home safely, but Mother never talked about it. I did not even know how he got home, and I knew better than to ask.

This brings me to September 1959, another dark period in Mom's life. Dad had been committed for the last ten years, since January 31, 1949, to a hospital way out of town. During those ten years, Mom made occasional trips by Greyhound Bus to visit him, bringing him pink boxes of Chinese char siu pork buns and packages of clean underwear. My sisters and I took turns accompanying Mom. Then on September 20, Mom received dreadful news that Dad had passed away there. I did not hear any of the details, but maybe Mom did not know or understood them either. My friend, Milton, whom I had dated during that summer, came from San Francisco to Oakland to hold my hand and to pay his condolences to Mom. After that visit, I never saw him again. A wake was held for Dad on October 25 at a mortuary in San Francisco, followed the next day with a funeral and a burial service at the Chinese Tung Sen Tong Cemetery in Colma, South San Francisco. I did not cry. His death certificate stated he died at age 61, but Mom clarified he was really 69–20 years older than she, who was age 49; I was 20. Dramatic as this was, that black cloud never came over me, nor ever again.

FEELING ALONE

He must have felt so alone
With nothing to do
But pace the floor
And wait for tomorrow

When will today end?
When will tomorrow come?
Only to wait
For another tomorrow

CHAPTER TWENTY-ONE:

NOT A DIME IN MY POCKET

Miraculously I earned around $800 during each of the three summers that I worked at Tai Ping. However, my total net take-home pay was never enough to cover the entire school year's expenses, so I took all kinds of odd jobs during the school year too.

At the start of each semester, from the time I was a sophomore at Cal, I worked on the registration lines at Sproul Hall, where new and returning students lined up for blocks with their IBM punch cards needed for the manual enrollment process. The pay was good, but the temporary job at Cal lasted only a few days during the registration period. After registration, wearing my "in fashion at the time" red Keds tennis shoes, I literally ran back and forth across campus to enroll for my classes. Nothing was more disastrous than when a class I needed was full, especially if it was a prerequisite to another class or one that was not offered often, which could affect the units needed for graduation. Timing for taking those classes was very important. I was determined, though, by showing up on the first day of classes with hopes that the instructor would add me to the roster—or replace me with someone who had dropped out. With some luck, or by hook and by crook, I would somehow make it into the class.

About halfway through the semester, I often ran short of

money. That was when I would make my daily trips at three o'clock, rain or shine, to the campus Placement Center at South Hall, located in the middle of campus, to join the line of students waiting for job referrals. If no appropriate requests came in for work I could do, I stretched what little money I had and checked again the following day. Some days I had only a dime in my pocket and wondered how I was going to make that last until my next job. I never, ever wanted to borrow money.

I did find odd jobs, like babysitting at a grammar school near Ashby and College Avenue while mothers attended the PTA meetings. Several times I helped serve and clean up at dinner parties for a professor on Hillegass Street on the Oakland-Berkeley border. After spending the night in her cozy guest bedroom, I headed by bus back to campus in the morning in the same clothes I had worn the day before.

The year my father died, 1959, was a tough year for me. Joanne had left Cal and Muriel also dropped out, leaving me on my own. I had no close friends, so I clung to Nancy Lee, Muriel's close friend from Oakland High. Nancy was sweet and pretty and had a bouncy, bubbly personality. She never had a bad hair day, and her skin was porcelain white. We had so much fun. In my senior year at Cal, Nancy had the family sedan and carpooled with me. Hers was my first long-lasting friendship with anyone. As long as I can remember, only once when I was in grammar school did Mom let me go play with a classmate who lived in our neighborhood. That was the first time I had a small bowl of pork and beans for a snack, and I liked it.

Every morning I boarded the bus on Foothill Boulevard, getting off at Telegraph and Bancroft avenues, and ran past Sproul and Dwinelle Halls straight to the Bancroft Library, hoping to find an empty spot at one of the long study tables on the second floor. Except for the hanging fluorescent lights that beamed down at the center of each table, the room was dark and cold, the ornate ceiling very high. The adjacent brightly lit reference room had drawers of file cards listing all the books in the library. I would leave two stacks of books on one of the tables—saving a spot for myself and one for my friend Nancy; or she would do the same for me if she arrived on campus first.

Nancy introduced me to her friends from Chinatown, Clifford Lew and Feegat Wong, and invited me over every New Year's Eve because I never had a date. And it was Nancy and I, using her older brother Dan's equipment, who taped music for the Chinese Students' Club Dances. Since we had taken a calligraphy course together (one of the few A's I received at Cal), we made the large posters that were displayed on easels at the brick entrance to Sather Gate to publicize our club events.

I was always tired. In the library, I would cross my arms on top of the study table, place my head on my arms and fall asleep. From hunching over the hard edge of the table, I would wake up feeling sick to my stomach and could not resume studying for hours. I suppose I did that to escape my troubles.

Nancy knew I slept a lot. If I was not in one of my classes or at the library, Nancy found me asleep in one of the cots at the women's lounge on the first floor of Wheeler Hall. One time when I was not scheduled to ride home with Nancy and had laid down for a quick nap, I awoke with a start to find no one around. It was pitch-black, past closing time; all the exit doors to the building were locked. Luckily I was able to release the lock from the inside so I could run for a bus on Telegraph Avenue. When I arrived home, Mom and my sisters had gone to bed. It was past midnight and I was starving, so I raided the refrigerator for leftovers.

Years later, Mom told me with a bit of a chuckle, "Oh, how you could eat everything in sight! One time I went to the refrigerator to take out the leftovers I knew I had saved the night before for dinner, but all the dishes were empty. You had helped yourself to all of it! And that was not the only time. Your favorite food was "sheen choi," marinated greens, or "gnow nam," beef stew meat with muscles and tendons! You would clean those up too!

Each semester after midterms and finals, the professors usually posted grades outside the classrooms. My hopes of transferring to U.C. Med Center in San Francisco to study dental hygiene were dashed when I received a "D" in Organic Chemistry and also a "D" in Subject A, better known as "Bonehead" English, in my second year. My faculty advisor warned me if I did not raise my grade point average, I would be placed on probation or be dropped from Cal. I quickly picked Home Economics as my new major and switched from the College of Letters and Sciences to the College of Agriculture. My grades did improve with fashion design, decorative arts, and languages (Italian and French), but I continued to struggle in Economic Statistics, Art History, Italian Literature, Psychology, and Business Law. I wondered if I would ever graduate.

I remember the time my final grade in Calligraphy was posted on the wall as a B. I could not believe it, since every assignment I turned in had received an A. I spoke to the professor immediately, who admitted his mistake and officially changed the grade to what I deserved. Besides, I needed the A to boost my Grade Point Average.

One Easter holiday I worked for Andreas Papandreou, Chairman of the Department of Economics at Cal. I babysat his four children the entire week while he and his wife attended a seminar or retreat out of town. I had no idea one day he would follow in his father's footsteps as Prime Minister of Greece. My claim to fame was that I had a part in potty-training his baby boy!

One time I found steady work cooking for an artist who had a separate art studio in the back of her house on the north side of campus. Every afternoon I rode the bus up Euclid Avenue to nearly the end of the line to her house, where the artist had placed her instructions, recipes and ingredients on the kitchen counter and expected a perfectly prepared meal for her and her husband. The strangest thing about cooking for her was using her large, crudely handmade ceramic pottery bowls in the oven for her casseroles. After serving dinner at six o'clock, I promptly caught the bus to the end of the line, where the driver made a U-turn and headed south back to campus. I would meet Nancy for dinner at the school cafeteria. My favorite food was meatloaf and mashed potatoes because they were soft and did not take long to chew and swallow. When I bought a serving of vegetables like cabbage, peas, string beans, canned corn, asparagus or broccoli, I topped the dish with free gobs of mayonnaise to make them more filling. Afterwards, Nancy and I returned to the second floor of the main library, where our stacks of books were waiting for us.

In my last year of school, I was lucky to find one of the few small, gray metal lockers that someone had just emptied out in the basement floor of the library. I put claims on it with my padlock, so for the rest of the year that was a load off my back! No more lugging everything on the bus, and my small wicker tote bag was even lighter!

Sometimes with only a dime in my pocket, I could only afford a small bag of potato chips for lunch at the Bear's Lair. Once, after politely offering it to my friends at the table, the bag was nearly empty. So much for lunch, I thought, as I reached in my purse for a lemon drop and popped it in my mouth. After that, if I was short of money, I would not join my friends for lunch. Instead, I would sneak across the walkway over to the Student Union, buy a bag of chips from the vending machine, sink into a big lounge chair and eat it all by myself. On rare occasions when we had a loaf of bread at home, I would pack four sandwiches with either tuna fish, deviled eggs, or a slice of lunchmeat, and eat one at a time throughout the day. I bet Mom wondered where all her bread went!

After Nancy introduced Feegat to me, he and I started double-dating with Nancy and Clifford. Feegat did the driving because he had a car. He was a Criminology student at Cal, and worked after school at Kwik Way Hamburgers (one of the earliest fast-food take-out joints) on Twenty-Second and Telegraph in Oakland and returned back on campus afterwards to study. I was really happy when Feegat showed up at the library with a bag of fried chicken and fries for me from Kwik Way. I don't know what gave him the idea I was still hungry, but he was thoughtful. On nights he offered me a ride home, I gladly took him up on it—along with my bag of food from Kwik Way. No refrigerator raids on those nights.

Every day I ran across campus from one class to another. I raced from Chemistry lectures (I had Nobel Peace Prize-winner Dr. Melvin Calvin for Organic Chemistry) in the 1,000-seat Wheeler Auditorium to the labs across campus, and then I would traipse back for lunch at the Bear's Lair, which was part of Stephens Hall. My friends and I sat at tables close to the jukebox, where neon lights in Lifesaver shades of yellow, red, orange and green perked me up. Sometimes the manager set the machine so we could play all the 45s we wanted without feeding a single nickel. I pushed every button for Frank Sinatra, Ella Fitzgerald, Bobby Darrin and Pat Boone, and then waited for the free handouts of 5-to-a-pack sample Winston and Salem cigarettes to come around so I could light one up later in the library hall and pretend I knew how to smoke.

Sometimes if our group felt like splurging, we would stop for hamburgers at Kip's on Bancroft. That was when I first noticed young students from the nearby School for the Deaf and Dumb, so inappropriately called then, huddled right up to the jukebox. Seeing the neon lights and feeling the strong vibrations of the bass beat, they tapped their feet and kept time to the music better than anyone with the gift of hearing.

One year Ed Lowe, a chap from Napa, and I double-dated with Michael Moy from Menlo Park and Nancy Foon from Suisun to the Big Game at the prestigious Stanford University in Palo Alto. Both football teams rivaled to see which would win the coveted "Axe." For other sporting events, Feegat took me to some of the intercollegiate basketball games, which were very exciting, especially in 1959, when our team that included Darrell Imhoff and Al Buck, won the NCAA title. But the most fun I had with Feegat was seeing foreign movies like "Two Women" with Sophia Loren, "Women in the Dunes," and Chushingura" or going dancing. I also prided myself for sneaking and going out with Richard, Feegat's friend from Kwik Way, because I knew Mom would not have approved of me dating a Caucasian. As far as she knew, Feegat was picking me up as his date–a little white lie.

In my last year at Cal, registration fees nearly doubled from my freshman year, to $45 a semester. That was the one and only time I approached Mom to borrow money (we had learned a long time ago not to ask for anything). Out of money and short on job referrals, I told the Dean of Women at Cal, I think her name was Katherine Towle, about my financial woes. She extended a no-red-tape personal loan to me without charging interest and did not stipulate when I had to repay it. Without her help, I probably would have dropped out, so I owe her my life. Seriously.

I was so tired of running for buses, classes, jobs and job referrals. As long as I can remember, since junior high, even my nose ran every day. I thought I had a year-round cold and carried tissues in my purse, but those did not last. I often raised my hand in class and headed for the girls' restroom to stuff as much toilet paper into my purse as I could, but that did not last either. For years I did not know that my runny nose, itchy throat, sneezing and watery eyes were due to seasonal allergies.

One time in college my legs and arms ached so badly, I ran up to Cowell Hospital on campus and complained of arthritis to the doctors. "Growing pains," said one doctor, and I believed him. That did not stop me from telling Nancy that whenever I felt those "growing pains," it was going to rain the next day. And it usually did.

All I wanted was to graduate, get a full-time job, stop running and move on with my life. As I heard someone say on television one night, "The money in my meter is running out." And I was running out of dimes.

CHAPTER TWENTY-TWO:

GROSVENOR PLACE

Spring 1961. I finished four years at Cal, struggled with school and was tired of rushing. I was, as one would say, "burnt out," and I needed to slow down, smell the roses and taste a few more lemon drops.

I satisfied all the requirements to earn my Bachelor of Science degree in Home Economics… except for one: I needed a class in American Institution-Political Science. Luckily, I had already taken American History to satisfy part of the requirement, but by taking Introduction to Government at Oakland's City College before summer's end, and transferring the units, I would be in the 1961 class of graduates at Cal. I could work a full-time job during the day, attend school at night and receive my diploma in June.

Tom Chinn, an old friend whom I knew from the Presbyterian Church in Oakland, was working at a small grocery store near the Kaiser Building by Lake Merritt. Al and Dorothy, owners of the market, made the world's best chicken salad sandwiches. At lunchtime, they did a brisk business from workers in nearby office buildings. Tommy mentioned a job a few blocks away at 362 Twenty-Second Street, where Mr. Bert Corona, owner of M.D. Francisco Interiors, was looking for an assistant to replace his long-time employee, Jayne Leong, who was leaving. Jayne was a classmate of Joanne's at Oakland High. The shop was on the ground floor of the El Dorado Building and across the street from the Bermuda Building in downtown Oakland, where Franklin Street runs north into Broadway.

The Bermuda Building, among many other structures in the Bay Area, was badly damaged during the devastating earthquake of 1989. Every window of the nine-story building was blown out, and the structure leaned lop-sided for nearly fifteen years before remodeling work began.

Employees from the Pacific Telephone Company occupied the offices above M.D. Francisco; many of them were his loyal customers. His small showroom displayed jewelry, furniture and accessories. Most of the sales were made through catalogs and sample books of carpets, drapery, fine jewelry and household items like Revere copper-bottom cookware, Franciscan fine china, and Dansk stainless steel flatware. In one corner were two display cases of diamond rings and jewelry. His father-in-law, a diamond dealer in Los Angeles, supplied him with the high-quality loose stones. I applied for the job and was hired.

Mr. Corona, a tall, handsome and charming Mexican man, taught me the business from the ground up as he spoke enthusiastically about fabrics, colors and textures. I could not learn the business fast enough to keep up with him, as he would frantically dash into the shop, blurt out some instructions to me, then scurry off and disappear down the street. One of his contracts was furnishing and decorating model homes and offices for a construction company, so the first thing I learned was how to measure rooms for drapery and wall-to-wall carpeting.

Mr. Corona often drove me to San Francisco in his noisy Volkswagen bus to transact business at the Western Merchandise Mart and the upscale decorators' shops at Jackson Square, a design center in San Francisco. His wife Blanche, daughter of the diamond dealer, was the bookkeeper. Between the two, I learned every aspect of a small business operation: sales, purchasing, shipping, accounts payable and receivable, payroll and sales tax reporting, customer service, and handling collections from deadbeat customers who bought on credit. As time went on, Mrs. Corona came less often to work, choosing to stay home when they moved further from Oakland. M.D. Francisco Interiors became a one-girl office, with me as the one girl and Mrs. Corona giving me instructions over the phone about how to handle sales and payroll tax reporting, because deadlines had to be met.

This was early 1961. Muriel was working as a secretary at Kaiser Aluminum a few blocks away and still dating Ricky, who would soon be receiving his civil engineering degree from Cal. Muriel and I often met for lunch at Al and Dorothy's market and ordered chicken salad sandwiches. Marilyn worked at Highland Hospital as a secretary and was applying to enter the Foreign Service, her dream and perhaps a chance to get away from home. Joanne and Dennis lived in Berkeley with their now two-year-old daughter Pamela. Vickie, a star student, finished Franklin Elementary School one block from our home and went on to take accelerated classes at Hamilton Junior High School.

About this time, Mom noticed that whenever we brought friends home (especially boyfriends), she could not serve company in the dining room because it was used as a bedroom. She knew this did not give our friends a good impression, and decided we needed a house with a dining room so we could seat and serve food to guests at a table. Once again, Mom solicited Marilyn's help in finding a house in a better neighborhood. This time we worked with a real estate agent, bubbly Edith Perreira, who gave us several listings and drove us to the ones we wanted to see. I remember one house in particular, as we all piled into Edith's car. It was a darling house on Trestle Glen Road in a beautiful neighborhood by the Lake, and we fell in love with it. However, by the time we wanted to present an offer, the house was already sold. We were very disappointed, but continued our search.

Another listing in the same neighborhood, but on

Grosvenor Place, came on the market. Ironically, this was the same intersection I had crossed on my way to a job interview with the Vickers! Mom purchased the lovely white stucco house in the beautiful Trestle Glen District, with tree-lined streets, lovely gardens and green lawns. What made our house special was a red Japanese maple tree next to a beautiful magnolia tree in our front yard. We had a dining room with large French windows where we would watch the bus pass right in front of our house on its way to downtown and San Francisco. *Mom seemed to pick homes with public transportation close to, if not right in front of, our house! She was so smart!*

I used my cost-plus-ten-percent discount at work to help Mom purchase wall-to-wall carpeting, custom-made draperies and a brown wood dining table set that could seat up to ten people, which made Mom really happy with her accomplishment. Little did I know at the time the reason for our move and Mom's real intentions. Mom sold the Eighth Avenue home for $13,500, which she had bought for $12,500, and paid $22,000 for our new three-bedroom home with a large living room, dining room, kitchen, bathroom, breakfast nook and big backyard. The attached garage with the double wooden garage door was perfect for Marilyn's '57 Chevy, and finally she had one of the three bedrooms all to herself! Mom and Vickie shared one of the two back bedrooms, while Muriel and I shared the other one across the hall. Kudos to Mom!

Besides moving into a new house, things were also looking up for me. I had a good job at M.D. Francisco, bought a Singer 403 portable sewing machine with the fancy cams for decorative stitches (I still use it today) and bought ALL the material I wanted to sew with. I bought my first pair of contact lens, and when my optometrist Dr. Clayton Soohoo (with an office on Eighteenth Street, around the corner from the Art Deco-style Fox Oakland Theater) popped them into my eyes and said, "Open your eyes slowly," I was amazed. A whole new world opened before me. Everything was crystal-clear and I could see without the aid of thick frames and lenses in front of my eyes. All the billboards, signs and street names came out even better than the time I got my first pair of eyeglasses in grammar school.

Now I ate all the chicken salad sandwiches I wanted, and had money to buy more lemon drops. There was much to celebrate, except for one thing… I did not have a boyfriend.

CHAPTER TWENTY-THREE:

DESPERATION

One day in early 1961, around January or February, the phone rang. It was my friend Feegat. After a few words of greeting and the usual "What's new?," he said, "My buddy Stanley just got discharged after serving three years in the Army, and there's a party for him this weekend. Come and be my guest at the party."

My heart started thumping, because his call meant I had a date for the upcoming weekend. I grinned from ear to ear. I liked Feegat, a slim handsome guy with a wonderfully outgoing personality; he was a year and a half older than I. In high school, he was the head cheerleader at Oakland Technical High School, so he must have been very popular with the students, but I did not know him at that time. Since meeting him in college through my friend Nancy, Feegat and I had been dating for two years, often double-dating with Nancy and Feegat's friend, Clifford Lew. Feegat was a wonderful dancer; he had a good sense of rhythm and natural moves, whether he was dancing swing, mambo or cha-cha. He was a great slow dancer too, as he often drew me close while we listened to Johnny Mathis sing, "Hold me close. Never let me go…" and my eyes would get misty as I tumbled into Dreamland.

Feegat and I were very good friends. We teased and said the funniest things about each other. Since I was so serious all the time, only a very special person could pull that opposite, funny side out of me like that. He was quick with words and witty, and we often laughed ourselves to tears. Sometimes just a couple of his words meant a whole lot to me.

"Miss me?" he would innocently ask as he lifted one eyebrow in a flirty manner.

"You can't imagine how," I'd tease back as we sparred words back and forth that got risqué and naughtier with each response. People who overheard us would give us puzzled or dirty looks, not understanding our sense of humor. We took none of it seriously… no, we never took each other seriously. No passion, no romance, not even a kiss. I wondered why. Was laughing and teasing just a way to cover up our true feelings about each other?

Many times I wanted to discuss our relationship, but I was afraid if I did, it would end our dating, and that I did not want to risk. He was not my boyfriend, no matter how badly I wanted to say he was. Real boyfriends and girlfriends exchange Valentine cards and gifts and go out together on New Year's Eve—we never did.

Feegat picked me up on Saturday for the party, given by Stanley's fiancée. They had been engaged for several months since his honorable discharge from the military service. I recognized him as the same Stanley I had met in the ninth grade at Lincoln Square when I was fourteen years old, the one several kids shouted repeatedly, "Stanley, Stanley, you be captain; yeah, you be captain." He was the one who picked me last on his team, and for that reason I did not like him.

I found out, much to my surprise, that Stanley and I shared the same birthday! He was born on March 27, 1939, at 10:10 p.m. in Oakland Chinatown, and an hour and a half later, in San Francisco Chinatown, I was born. (Many married couples have the same birth date, but being born on the same year is rare, so we are pretty unique.) Anyway, I had a good time at the party, since many of my friends were there.

As Feegat and I stood on my old, gray wood front porch at the end of the evening after the party to say goodnight, I fumbled for my keys and thanked him for a great time. He drove off in his white 1960 Pontiac Bonneville. He, the one who took me to Cal basketball games and brought me take-out dinners in a paper bag from Kwik Way, remained a perfect gentleman, much to my dismay.

A few weeks later, toward the end of March, I was invited to another celebration, this time at a private house in San Francisco, for Stan's birthday. As the lights dimmed and the cake was brought out to the party-goers, the decoration said, "Happy Birthday, Stan and Fran!" The celebration was a surprise for me too! I was shocked, then embarrassed, but thankful that the group directed most of their attention toward outgoing and friendly Stanley. I was not used to anyone celebrating my birthday.

Then in June, when my family had moved into our new house on Grosvenor Place in the Trestle Glen area, the phone on the wall in the breakfast nook rang. "I'll get it," I shouted, knowing full well the call was probably not for me. As I reached for the phone, I sat down on one of Mom's gray chrome dinette chairs in the breakfast nook.

"Hello," I said. "Who? Stanley Gim? Oh yes, I do remember meeting you, at your, uh, our, birthday party in March." (pause)

"No, Muriel is not home right now." (pause)

"I see. You want to know if she is busy this Saturday because you want to take her to a movie?"

I thought for a moment. Muriel was "going steady" with Ricky, so that meant they were seeing only each other and not dating anyone else. I quickly responded, "Yes, uh, she's busy, but I am not!"

I know, speaking out like that was bold of me, but what I said about Muriel was true, and I was desperate for my own date. Growing up, I was brainwashed with the idea that I must marry and produce lots of kids. At 22, I was already old and not even close to having a boyfriend, so how was I to fulfill those expectations?

Evidently Stan had broken off his engagement over

religious differences with his fiancée, who was a Catholic convert. She was adamant that their children be brought up in the Catholic faith and that he start Catechism classes at her church. Stan grew up going to an Episcopal Church in Chinatown; he did not agree, and refused to sign the necessary papers taking that oath. Their engagement was off, and she gave back her ring with the sparkling diamond.

Stan and I continued to date after that first movie, often double-dating with Muriel and Ricky, Nancy and Clifford or Feegat and his date, June Yamane. We were just one happy family of friends.

One time Feegat was my date and June was Stan's date, since none of us were serious about each other like Muriel and Ricky were. As the four of us were walking down the street, I suddenly realized that Feegat had disappeared with June, stranding me with Stan. We had no idea where they were, and when we finally caught up with them, they were around a corner, snickering and laughing hysterically like two kids playing tricks on us. They had managed to purposely ditch us, for whatever reasons, and so I was stuck with Stan. How rude of them!

Luckily, Stan and I got along and had enough to talk about, so we became even better acquainted and continued seeing each other. Stan was not such a bad guy after all! We went to places in San Francisco like the Purple Onion off Broadway, Finocchio's (where gorgeous-looking men with beautiful bodies impersonated women), the Tonga Room at the Fairmont Hotel and the Top of the Mark at the Mark Hopkins Hotel. We saw sexy torch singer Lena Horne and Mel Torme (the Velvet Fog) in the Carnelian Room of the Fairmont Hotel, and attended shows featuring singer Nancy Wilson and comedienne Rusty Warren. We saw jazz greats Dave Brubeck and Peggy Lee at the Masonic Temple and we went nightclubbing at the Rickshaw on Waverly Place, where Abe Batat was the featured jazz pianist and where I nursed one drink all night—a King Alphonse over the rocks with cream—made with Kahlua (coffee-flavored liqueur) over ice cubes with a splash of cream. If we were in San Francisco, no matter how late the evening was, we could always drop into Sam Wor's for *Siu Yeh,* a midnight snack, and say hello to one of the popular waiters, Edsel.

One evening, Stan and I ventured into a topless joint in North Beach, where a "Go Go" dancer in really high heels stood on top of the long wooden table where we sat and wildly swung in circles the tassels pasted on her nipples. Watching her was not the only thing that made me woozy that evening!

Stan and I patronized my old stomping grounds, the Log Cabin in South San Francisco, but he didn't have a clue as to what kind of music was playing, what the dance tempo was and how to keep the beat. However, he was a thoughtful and generous guy with a friendly attitude.

The first time Stan took me out to dinner, we dined at No. 9 Fisherman's Grotto at the foot of Taylor Street at San Francisco's Fisherman's Wharf. I eyed the Lobster Thermidor on the menu, but for $3.20, that selection was the second most expensive dinner choice. Mom had taught us not to be greedy, so for seventy cents less, I opted for the fresh grilled sea bass with French fries and salad. Stan had scallops sautéed in wine a la Newburg, which was also $2.50 on the menu. I was still working on my salad when he had finished his entire dinner. He lit up a cigarette and watched me eat. I ate even slower as he lit up another cigarette, which left residue on his fingers that I could smell the rest of the evening. I was tempted to have a piece of cheesecake for dessert, but for fifty cents, the price was far too expensive, and besides, it would have taken me forever to eat it, even if I had shared it with him.

When Stan and I went out one night to Bella Napoli, an Italian restaurant on Telegraph Avenue in Oakland, I ordered spaghetti as my entree. I figured I would order something soft and easy to swallow so that I could keep up with "Fast-Eating" Stan (he did everything fast). Out came a generous bowl of spaghetti from the kitchen, sort of family-style, with a large serving spoon. I ate as much as I could, until the waiter finally came to our table and asked if I was done. Of course I was. Couldn't the waiter see that most of it was consumed? He took the bowl away and then out came this big platter of spaghetti, my entree! Apparently the first course was soup with spaghetti noodles! Stan and I looked at each other, and my mouth fell open in shock. Another plate of food would have taken me the rest of the night to eat, not to mention how full I was, ready to burst out of my girdle.

I was too embarrassed to ask for a "doggie bag," so my order went back into the kitchen, wasted. I never could eat fast. Never, because I mull over each bite and savor each flavor. The size of every bite is eyeballed and calculated (and preferably weighed), and every bite is precious.

I continued attending my night classes at Oakland City College, and when my course credits were transferred to Cal, I was officially in the graduating class of June 1961. No one I knew came to my graduation, not even me. I could not afford the rental fees for the cap and gown after buying the hardbound blue-cover yearbook, wallet-size graduation photographs, a tiny sterling silver class ring and, of all things, when I could least afford $90, a lifetime membership in the Cal Alumni Association. I received an official document in the mail, signed by Edmund G. Brown, then Governor of California and President of the Regents, and Clark Kerr, President of the University of California, for my Bachelor of Science degree in Clothing Design.

I managed to finance and finish four years of college, and I fulfilled my dream. It was time to make bigger and better things happen in my life.

CHAPTER TWENTY-FOUR:

STAN THE MAN

Born in Oakland Chinatown on March 27, 1939, to For and Gladys Gim, Stanley (Stan) was the youngest (and the last to leave home)of seven children: sisters Peggy, Hazel, Annabelle, Lillian and Maybelle, and third-born brother, John. They lived on Sixth Street between Jackson and Madison. Being born on the same day as I, he too was welcomed into the Chinese Lunar Year of the Rabbit and under the Zodiac sign of Aries. According to Chinese calendars, the rabbit is honest, elegant and peace-loving, with impeccable manners. We are also intelligent in business, with a creative mind.

The Internet lists Aries—the Ram—as the first sign of the Zodiac, and includes persons born between March 21 and April 20. We are courageous, enthusiastic, energetic, confident, dynamic, assertive and outspoken, and we make things happen. On the other hand, we are impatient and impulsive, and we like to take risks. Wow! Pretty true, I think.

As soon as Stan graduated from high school in January 1957, he went straight to the U.S. Army Recruiting Office in Downtown Oakland to enlist. However, because of the minimum age requirement of 18, the Army could not sign him up without his mother's written consent. On March 29, just two days after he turned 18, he marched down to the recruitment office, took his shots and a physical, got a haircut, picked up his uniforms and soon after left for the training grounds at Fort Ord in Monterey, California. Leaving home turned out to be one of the biggest turning points in his life… growing up.

Stanley attended basic boot camp training at Fort Lewis, Washington, trained in electronics at Fort Mammoth, New Jersey, and received advanced training in guided missiles at the Aberdeen Proving Grounds in Maryland. He was transferred to Vicenza, Italy, and then went on to Pirmasens, Germany, where he received his final training in nuclear warhead maintenance. Everywhere he went, he met soldiers from all over the United States. With every opportunity, he traveled—visiting Verona, Pisa, Udine, Rome, Trieste and Venice. With time off for being "Soldier of the Month" (for spit-shiny shoes), he met up with an old buddy from high school, Elton (Al) Fong, who was also stationed in Germany. Together they toured Naples and Rome and both walked to the top of the Leaning Tower of Pisa, which was allowed at that time. The highlight of that trip for Stan was visiting the Vatican and seeing Mt. Vesuvius, an ancient volcano.

Branching away from home gave Stan a broad exposure to the real world. He gained a different perspective of life outside the Chinatown ghetto, where large, tight-knit Chinese families dealt only with each other in a safe community environment, doing the same cultural things. By moving away, he saw how other people's lives were so different from that to which he was accustomed. By the same token, he was naïve to think he could trust everyone, like he could in his old Chinatown neighborhood, like those to whom he loaned money from his meager monthly earnings of $105.

After his three-year tour of duty ended in January 1960, Stan returned home… and his mother resumed putting out his clean clothes and socks every morning and packing his black metal lunch pail and coffee thermos for work. Whenever his dad made chicken, fish or pork chops for dinner, his mom made sure she removed every piece of bone in sight on Stanley's plate so there would be no chance of him choking on a bone. What a contrast to me, learning to lick a piece of fish without swallowing a single sliver of bone. Leaving home, serving time in the Army, learning to do everything for himself and experiencing good and bad lessons did not convince his mother to stop spoiling him. By now he knew he was perfectly capable of taking care of himself. "Really, Ma, I can do all this myself," he wanted to tell her.

After working a few months at Hoy Chang's on Eighth Street in Chinatown, earning $2.15 an hour as a stock clerk in a warehouse that carried paper products, gum, candy and cigarettes for small businesses, Stan's sister Peggy's husband, Henry Leong, found him a "real job" at Stecher-Traung, a lithography firm on Battery Street in San Francisco. Hired by John Christy, Stan started in May 1960 as a general worker at $9 an hour, mixing and preparing 50-pound pans of ink for the printing presses. Cleanup was hazardous, as he had to wipe each knife blade that was used in stirring batches of ink. He scrubbed ink pans that had been soaking in a vat of 160-degree caustic lye and, although he wore thick gloves that covered his arms, he was exposed to harsh chemicals and cleaning solvents. Fine particles of red, yellow, blue, green and black ink powders constantly blew in his work area, sprinkled down and stayed lodged in his hair even after he showered twice a day—once at work and again at home. Every night his pillowcase was dotted with the colors of confetti. Working with his bare hands in the cleaning solvents and chemicals toughened his hands and badly chapped his fingers.

The first time we held hands, his chapped hands felt like metal bristles from a bottle brush cutting into my hands. His fingertips were rough and stained like an automobile mechanic's hands… permeating the smell of smoke and ash from smoking cigarettes, and camouflaging the wonderful and sexy-smelling Old Spice cologne he was wearing.

A year later, he was promoted to millman and earned $13 an hour. There was plenty of overtime work in the printing industry, and his job paid well, with union and medical benefits. This was better than all the jobs he had held in the past.

As a young man, one of Stan's next-door neighbors was Mr. Henry Lee Ow Foo, a short-order cook at a café at Seventh and Broadway that catered to the longshoremen. For Stan's part in busing tables and washing dishes by hand each Saturday, he earned fifty cents an hour for three hours and received lunch: a hamburger steak, with mashed potatoes and green peas. Then, for helping out Manager Jerry Housley at the Oakland Tribune Distribution Center, at Ninth and Harrison (now the Lyons Building), sort and count bundles of newspapers for the local paperboys to take on their daily bike routes, Stan received free movie passes to the T & D Theater at Ninth and Broadway. Not bad, since his siblings constantly claimed he was a bad boy and a brat! And to this day, some of them still remind me what a rascal he was. Being the baby of the family, and a boy at that, he was very spoiled by his mother. When he was a young boy, he would throw tantrums when he did not get his way!

Stan's backyard neighbor, Mrs. Ong, mother of Marianne, George, James and Stan Ong, owned the Victory Grocery Store on Eighth, between Broadway and Franklin Streets. Every day at 5 p.m., Stan assisted her in closing up shop: covering the crates of fresh fruits and vegetables with tarp, locking up the cigarettes and watching her count the cash. Promptly at 7 p.m., he escorted her home, the bundle of cash tucked tightly under her arm. He did this for about eight months and made 75 cents an hour.

In college, my sister Joanne worked at Peralta Hospital on Thirtieth between Telegraph and Broadway, better known as "Pill Hill", where Merritt and Providence Hospitals were located just blocks away. From what I remember, she had fun working alongside the Chinese kids from the different Oakland schools. At that time I wanted to work there too, but I was not as lucky as Joanne to land a job there.

When I heard Stan had also worked at Peralta Hospital during high school, I asked him one day what it was like working there. "Well," said Stan, "I arrived at the hospital after high school at 3:45, changed into a server's white jacket and hat, and ate my dinner from food that was leftover from the lunch menu. My absolute favorites were 10-to-12-inch-long turkey wings, where the meat was so juicy and tender, it fell right off the bones! Other kids working with me, under supervision by the night dietician, were Al, Wilson, Barbara, Nina, Beverly, Eva, and Feegat, to name a few. While some students prepared trays of food assembly-line style according to the patients' prescribed meal cards, others delivered the trays to the patients on the different floors by using a dumbwaiter and conveyor belts.

"My shift started at 4:15 as a floater and, depending where I was needed, I covered one of five food stations: soup, salad, hot meals, dessert and beverage, replenishing each as quantities ran low. As the trays were returned to the kitchen, I helped sanitize the dishes and flatware in an industrial washer. While some students headed home an hour later, my shift did not end until 7 p.m. One of my duties was to help clean the ovens, coffee urns and large vats, as well as the two heavy 36" x 40" commercial grade pans, and put away the trays and silverware.

"The last thing I did was assist Willie, the janitor, in collecting and placing garbage into two heavy 40-gallon industrial steel cans, load them both onto a heavy-duty cart, and transport them in a service elevator to the dumpster, several flights down, on the same floor as the morgue, to a refrigerator unit, where the cans were stored overnight for the next morning's pickup. The area was freezing cold and eerie. Once in a while, if there was an overflow of bodies in the morgue, I could see the shape of a corpse under a sheet on a gurney in the hall, waiting to be taken the next day to a funeral parlor.

"After working there about a year and a half, I left to work at Kwik Way Hamburgers, one of the early fast food joints, on 21st and Telegraph, across from the YMCA. By then, Feegat had also left Peralta to work at Kwik Way.

Looking back now, it was exciting working at Peralta."

"I also knew Feegat when he worked at Kwik Way," I chimed in, "because occasionally he would bring me fried chicken and French fries in a Kwik Way bag when I stayed late at Cal to study. That was very thoughtful of him. What was your job there?"

"I was the deep-fry potato cook. The French fries were made of real potatoes, and each order included a small container of catsup mixed with horseradish. The manager on duty—most of the time it was either Feegat or a guy named Rankin—usually did the grilling of the hamburgers. I helped pre-mix 10-to-14 milkshakes—chocolate, strawberry or vanilla—at a time for the freezer, then I fried shrimp or helped batter chicken in buttermilk and seasoned flour. I worked there about a year until I graduated from high school and enlisted in the Army. Guys I knew, Ricky Chinn and John Tong, worked at another Kwik Way location by the Grand Lake Theater. Now you know the rest of my story."

Stan was a morning person. No matter how late he stayed up, he arose at five every morning. He was never late to his job in San Francisco, never late to anything. If he did not arrive at his destination an hour early, he considered himself late.

I was the opposite. When Stan came over on the weekends in his Ford Falcon, I would still be in bed in the back bedroom I shared with Muriel. "Couldn't you come a little later so I can sleep in longer?" I asked him over and over again as I turned away to the other side.

Growing up in a house full of women, I had never seen anyone so energetic. His normal pace was three times faster than a marathon runner. He did not work out or "pump iron," yet his arm muscles were enormous and hard as granite. He was not the scrawny kid in the comic book advertisements who had sand kicked in his face. There was nothing he could not do physically, like the day he ripped out all the overgrown bushes and trees in Mom's backyard as if they were twigs. I hoped that impressed her, because it certainly impressed me.

Stan was ready to settle down and pack his own lunchbox.

PRINCE CHARMING

Prince Charming is at my doorstep
Sweeping me off my feet
Like White Knight in the old movies
Wearing armor shiny and sleek

He grabs me by my waistline
Tosses me on his horse
Whispers softly into my ears
"Hang on, while we ride the course"

Our four legs are dangling
Several feet off the ground
I feel faint so I plead with him
Please, dear Prince, put me down!

What can I say, what can I do
I am four feet off the ground
I'm getting dizzy, and dizzier
Going up and down and around

My fear of heights comes over me
But my fear of falling is greater
Okay, Okay, now put me down
Before I change my answer

But not before we disappear
Into the golden sunset
To be together forever and ever
Until one of us kicks the bucket

This poem was co-winner of the first place award for the Rossmoor TV Channel 28 Valentine Poetry Contest, February 2014.

CHAPTER TWENTY-FIVE:
GOOD ENOUGH

In September1961, Stan approached Mom, who was standing by the stove preparing lunch—probably her famous macaroni and cheese—and asked her permission to marry me. We were each 22 years old and mature, with good jobs: Stan earned more than $400 a month and I, close to $300. We had no reason to wait, so with Mom's nod of approval, we brought our plates of macaroni to the dining room, sat at Mom's new walnut-brown dining table that could extend to seat ten people, and ate lunch while we proceeded with our wedding plans for December—just three months away.

I told Stan about the debts I had: a college loan, a life insurance policy an agent cleverly conned me into buying while I was in college, and major upcoming dental expenses. So many events had happened to me that year, like graduating from college, getting a job and meeting Prince Charming. It did not matter to me that Stan was *See Yup* and did not speak our Cantonese dialect, something I always knew Mom preferred. On the one hand, I wanted to please Mom, but on the other hand, I wanted to choose for myself. I certainly did not want her to tell me whom to marry. What mattered most was that Stan was an honest, hard-working, friendly person with fine qualities, a jolly great attitude… and muscles, really hard ones!

Maybe someday Mom would realize that Stan was good enough for her daughter. Stan promised to take care of me—and my bills. I had no reason to doubt him. Absolutely none.

Stan showed me the sparkling, ¾-karat, marquis-cut, solitaire diamond ring. I glanced at it, coddled the ring in the palm of my hand for a few seconds and said, as I placed it back in his hands, "It is beautiful, but I am not the diamond type." He frowned, having spent $800 for it last year, but he said no problem. He would return the ring to the jeweler who sold it to him for his first engagement. Certainly, he would recover at least the cost of the ring.

I really did not want a ring he had chosen for another woman, and also, I did not want him to spend that much money on me. Besides, why bother with a ring when our engagement period would end in a couple of months? Instead, I ordered a pair of matching 14K solid white-gold wedding bands from M.D. Francisco's—$13 for Stan's, $12 for mine, including engraving on mine that said "S.G. loves F.F. 12-3-61." Following advice from Stan's dad, who told him not to keep the ring, Stan returned it to the jeweler. I did not learn until many months later that he recovered only $500. Stan and I were too young to understand the value of jewelry, antiques and real estate, which generally appreciate in value. I could kick myself for not keeping that beautiful ring; in hindsight, we were naïve, foolish and stupid. We were thinking only of the joy of getting married.

We picked December 3rd for our wedding date because the number three, or any multiples of three, like in our mutual birth date, 3-27-39, was our lucky number. We received approval from Stan's father, who read in the *Tung Shun* Ancient Chinese Almanac that it was indeed a good date. This daily guide, which originated over 4,000 years ago, has been published annually for more than 1,200 years and is now available in English. A different version claimed that one can "capitalize on good luck, minimize bad luck, improve career opportunities and improve relationships."

Stan and I agreed to marry in the First Christian Church in

Oakland at Twenty-Ninth and Fairmount because that was where Stan's older brother, John, married Evelyn Fong of Alameda four years earlier, on March 17, 1957. I loved the aisle that ran down the center of the sanctuary—it was the longest aisle I had ever seen in any church. Our invitations were written in Chinese and English, and printed on red card stock with traditional gold lettering. We invited over 400 guests, most of whom belonged to the Chin clan living in the Bay Area (Stan's father's surname was really Chin, but he came to America in the early 1920s with fake papers under the last name Gim).

On November 10, 1961, one month before the wedding, my two appointed bridesmaids, Nancy Lee and Stan's sister Lillian, hosted a lingerie bridal shower for me at my home on Grosvenor Place. Nancy, in her unique "curlicue" handwriting, requested invitees to RSVP to her home phone. About 25 of my friends in attendance at my shower caught me saying silly things like, "I cook anything but American food," "I'm gonna let Stan wear this for me," and "What are these? They are supposed to be longer!"

I selected off-white peau de soie satin material for my wedding gown. It was scoop-necked and short-sleeved, with a floor-length skirt pleated and fitted at the waist. Floral lace appliqués adorned the detachable double-panel train, which I designed. White gloves, a cascade of white baby roses and stephanotis, a pair of tear-drop pearl earrings, white satin heels and a small white Holy Bible completed my outfit. Muriel, my maid of honor, and my two bridesmaids wore knee-length dresses made of iridescent green-blue taffeta matching the style of my bridal dress. I thought Nancy, who also majored in clothing design at Cal, and I did a superb job tailoring these dresses. Stan's mom wore a light blue brocade dress, and my mom wore a stunning champagne-beige brocade dress with a brown fur collar, small hat to match, jade pendant, white gloves and ruby-red lipstick.

On the day of our wedding, my hairdresser, Mr. Phillip, a stocky, jovial, mustached Mexican fellow with a beauty salon on Park Boulevard, and later on MacArthur, came to our house early in the morning and coifed my hair.

Our best man Feegat Wong, groomsmen Ricky Chinn and John (Stan's brother), and the two ushers, Clifford Lew and Jerry Moy (Stan's cousin), wore white tuxedo jackets and black trousers. Fu-Yi, my friend from college who called me Mama Frances, was in charge of the guest book.

Stan, alias Mr. Clean, accidentally cut his right thumb that morning while he was washing his new midnight-blue Ford Falcon, but that did not keep him from beaming, along with me, the entire day. Dr. Thomas Toler officiated. The buffet reception, with traditional Chinese fare of chow mein, spareribs, roast pork, ham and fried chicken, was held in the church hall downstairs. We barely got around to greeting the hundreds of guests before it was time to serve champagne and cut our four-tier wedding cake and two sheet cakes, supplied by Neldam's Danish Bakery on Telegraph. The cakes cost a hefty $72.90.

Our professional photographer, Jack Chinn, who had a studio on Grand Avenue, was one of the first photographers to cover a wedding using Kodak's new color film, thus creating for us one of the first 3"-x-3" color photo albums along with our standard large black-and-white album. As Stan and I descended the church steps, we were showered with raw grains of rice, a Western tradition no longer permitted because of the hazard of people slipping on them and birds choking on them.

Mom told me recently she cried at my wedding. She was happy for Stan and me, but in her Chinese way of thinking, a girl marries out of her family into the boy's family and may not come home again. Mom could not bear to lose a daughter. I was the first of her five daughters she witnessed marrying, and it touched her deeply, but I did not see her crying that day. I did not know she felt that way.

Immediately following our wedding, we drove off in Feegat's white Pontiac Bonneville to our small, one-bedroom, rented apartment on the second floor of the six-unit building at Foothill and Sixth Avenue, where I changed into a red dress and a traditional black "*kwa*" embroidered satin jacket. We hopped into Stan's Falcon and raced down to the Gim residence on Sixth and Jackson across from Highway 17 (now the I-880 Nimitz Freeway), where his family members gathered. Stan and I served individual cups of tea to his parents and to each relative to show our respect. In return, they gave us money in *lee see* (or *hoan how)* red envelopes to wish us luck and happiness. On that day, my knight in shining armor came down from his white horse and swept me off my feet. His Band-Aid stuck out like a sore thumb, but on that day, it did not seem to bother him. We were both very happy.

We went to Carmel, Monterey and Sausalito for our honeymoon, driving right into the sunset, just as I had dreamed, cried and prayed for all those years. The entire day was like a fairy tale come to life, in which we did indeed find that "*Somewhere over the rainbow...trouble melts like lemon drops, away above the chimney tops."* And I was perfectly happy with my plain wedding band that matched Stan's. Time will tell if I can prove to my mom that Stan is good enough for me.

CHAPTER TWENTY-SIX:

TIME TO SAY GOODBYE

Mom, I often think of you leaving your homeland, China, in 1935. You were brave. You survived the long voyage across the Pacific Ocean. Twice I came close to drowning in deep waters, but I too survived. You did not know that about me.

I think of you caged up like an animal on Angel Island for two months, pacing back and forth in your cell. I too felt trapped with the families I worked for. Theirs was a different world. They provided a roof over my head, but promised no future for me. I would lie in bed and stare up at the white ceiling, watching black floaters inside my eyes squiggle and dance in quick circles. Like me, they moved around but went nowhere, trapped inside my eyes.

Silence is not golden. So little was said between us. Each time I went away, you never said goodbye. Did it ever hurt you to see my sisters and me, one by one, leave home? For nearly ten years, you had no idea where I lived or what I did, but did you care, or think about me? I questioned a lot in silence. Did you know for many nights I cried myself to sleep? Did you know I cried when a friend no longer loved me? Now I know you cared for me and my sisters, because everything you did, you did for us. I realize now you never said goodbye because you were busy at work and planning how to make a better life for us. What sacrifices you made!

I think of the times I was hungry; you must have felt hunger pangs then too. I saw you divide what little you had and give us the meat while you licked the bones. Eventually, I learned to lick the bones because that was where the most flavors were and the meat was most tender.

How many times were you short on money, afraid to apply for welfare for fear we would be deported? Some days I had only a dime in my pocket. Do you recall the money I borrowed from you when I was in college? I still owe you that, plus a whole lot more.

I now understand the hardships you went through and the sacrifices you made. You could have abandoned us, but you didn't. You remained strong. Each time you bought a house, you were providing a better place for us to live because you really cared about us.

Well, Mom, I'm writing this chapter for you. Some of the poems I have written reflect the anger and hurt I felt at the time the events were happening, but I am no longer angry at you, because harboring anger does not do us any good. I told you, if there was anything I said or did to hurt you all these years, like the time I blurted out in anger that you did not raise me, I am sorry.

Thank you for telling me your stories, and I hope you enjoy hearing mine. I, too, am glad you did not marry that pilot, who is now in Taiwan, because more than likely neither one of us would be here today in *Gum San* – Gold Mountain of America. You are truly a great lady. A wonderful mom.

Remember the other day when I mentioned lemon drops? You chuckled and said, "Oh, I liked lemon drops too! I bought them so that once in a while I could reach into the jar and give each of you one as a treat." One day you discovered they were all gone and wanted one of us to admit to the crime. I now confess I was the one who stole the lemon drops, but maybe you knew all along it was I.

I admit each time I paused on the sidewalk as I was leaving home to work for the rich white families, I wondered where you were. Maybe it hurt you too much to see me go, so you would rather not come out to say goodbye to me. You told me you cried at my wedding, and maybe, as you watched me ride away from the church with Stan, you felt you had lost me to his family. You have not. When I leave, I'll be gone for only a while and then I will come back. I like being your third daughter. Being stuck in the middle means something unique to me.

If Stan and I have children (at one time I thought having five girls would be so cool), I am sure I would raise them differently than how I was raised. That is just the way it is, as times and events around the world change and we grow and mature. My children will do the same when they have children of their own and choose how to nurture them, and their times will be very different from when we raised them.

Now I am back visiting Mom in her apartment at the Rose of Sharon by Lake Merritt in Oakland. She is in her 90s. A few hours later I left her apartment, with the delicious aroma in the hall of someone's cooking, stepped into one of the two elevators and pushed the button for the first floor. "Goodbye, Mom. I'll be back soon for another visit."

I reached inside my purse and pulled out a small round tin, took out a lemon drop and popped it into my mouth. They are still my favorite candy.

YOU NEVER SAID GOODBYE

You never said goodbye
I never saw you cry
All the times I left you
You never said goodbye

Tell me you are sorry
And sad to see my go
Tell me things will be all right
I really need to know

I do not want to go, Mom
But no one is telling me not to
Did you ever cry for my sisters
As one by one they left you?

Let us come inside your world
Don't keep us locked away
Like you did when we kids
Stealing away to play

Unlock the lock, unchain the door
Take us to the park
You don't need to face the world
Alone and in the dark

Let us cry together
Together we will survive
To face each day's new challenges
I'm just glad I'm alive

Like me you were born a daughter
Didn't you feel the pain?
Things that once were said to you
Were said with such disdain

Don't you know it's just a ploy
By men to keep us down
Like bound-footed women in China
Bounded to the ground?

Hold your own head high, Mom
As you have taught us to
Never mind what men have said
We are proud of you

I am eternally grateful
I've learned so much from you
Maybe someday my own children will feel
The same thoughts I feel about you

CHAPTER TWENTY-SEVEN:

MOMMY WE KNOW

After living at the Rose of Sharon for close to 30 years, and no longer able to continue living by herself, Mom moved in with my sister Muriel Luck, who was living at the Summerset Retirement Community in Brentwood, California, about an hour drive east of Oakland. Mom was 97 years old, and I, also a resident of Summerset with Stan, continued my visits with her. Muriel took great care of Mom as her health progressively got worse due to old age, though her mind was still very sharp to the end.

Mom spent about 10 days at Kaiser Hospital Sand Creek in Antioch before being transferred to the Bruns House in Alamo for hospice care. In less than twenty-four hours, my Mom, Susie Oy Lum Fong, passed away of natural causes on September 26, 2008, at the age of 98 (99 by Chinese standards). She wanted to live to 100. During her final days at Kaiser, she whispered to me, in her weakened voice, two things that will forever stick in my mind: "God will take care of me," and "I am a good person."

These were my parting words spoken at her funeral at the Albert Brown Funeral Home in Oakland on October 1, 2008, before she was buried a few blocks away at the Mountain View Cemetery in Oakland:

"Mommy, I remember. The year was 1942. Marilyn was six years old, Joanne was four, I was three and Muriel two.

We were living in Chinatown San Francisco and on Sundays you sent us to see Chinese movies while you stayed home to sew, or was it to iron our pretty little dresses? You taught us to hold hands tight and to look both ways before crossing the streets, and you warned us to be careful. You kept us safe. You washed our clothes by hand and carried four loads of laundry and cloth diapers up two stories to the roof to use the clotheslines before other tenants beat you to them.

"Later you heard stories about young Chinese girls becoming prostitutes, eloping, or running around with bad people, doing bad things. You did not want us to do that, so you moved us across the bay to a four-unit apartment house in West Oakland, where you were so proud to find a home for us with rental income that would help with your monthly payments. You kept a roof over our heads. You were even more proud when you paid off the mortgage within a year.

"In 1948, Vickie joined us as your fifth daughter. You moved us to a pair of flats out in the Avenues to get us into a better school district. While I was in college, you purchased a house in the Trestle Glen area of Lakeshore, because you were concerned that when we brought our boyfriends home, we did not have a dining room with a table to seat our guests. You wanted to give our friends a better impression of where and how we lived. How else was I going to find a doctor or a lawyer to marry?

"We remember you unselfishly gave us the pieces of meat to eat while you licked the bones of the fish heads. One time I complained that one of my sisters got a bigger piece of cake than I did. You said, 'Go ahead, weigh it.' I would have, but we did not have a scale. You taught us to share and to treat others with fairness. Just like the time you sat us down and divided your pieces of fine jewelry. You explained why Marilyn was to have your oldest and most valuable piece of jade because she was the oldest, and the first to go to work and give you part of her earnings. I was fortunate you gave me your diamond wedding rings, which you yourself bought and paid for, because you said when I got married, I only wanted a plain gold wedding band from Stan.

"I remember the time you bought a heavy 9-x-12 area rug from the Alameda Flea Market. Oh, how you loved to shop for bargains! Somehow you managed to get the rug home on the bus to your Rose of Sharon apartment, where you used it as padding while you did your daily tai chi exercises. You taught us to be thrifty and healthy. You know, because you lived for years with painful arthritis, gout, only one good eye and one kidney, yet you did not complain.

"We remember you always encouraged us to study hard. Reading and education were always on the top of your list of things to do. For me, that was my ticket out of living in poverty and performing domestic work for the rest of my life. You were smart. You were strong and determined. You were amazing and classy–like wearing your hats, gloves, high-heel shoes and ruby red lipstick!

"You always loved us. We love you for your devotion and years of hard work. You did a great job, Mommy. We know, and we will never forget you. Thank you."

After I spoke, my younger sister Vickie stood up and spoke her eloquent departing words to Mom, which included in part the following: "She was a REAL woman warrior, facing the challenges of raising a big family of women as a single mother. She taught each of my sisters and me to be strong, independent, and resourceful. But as an individual, she will be remembered for her enduring grace, dignity and strength."

By the way, Mom, don't worry. After over 50 years of marriage (and still going strong), Stan has proven he really is good enough for me.

EPILOGUE

Let me bring you up to date. It is now Year 2014, twenty years since I responded to a small ad in a local newspaper and attended an evening class in Alameda, Writing Circles for Women, which spear-headed me to write *Lemon Drops*.

After Stanley and I married in 1961, we rented an apartment on Foothill Boulevard and 6th Avenue in Oakland, then one a few blocks away on 8th Avenue and E. 18th Street. Since my sister Marilyn was in Washington D. C. at that time to train for the Foreign Service and Muriel, always the adventurous one, was working at the United States Embassy in London, Stan and I moved in with my mom on Grosvenor Place in 1963. While living at my mom's, I gave birth in 1964 to our son, Brandon Perry Gim. Within a year, Stan and I had saved $5,000 as a down payment toward a $22,000 house on Tiffin Road in the Upper Fruitvale/Dimond District of Oakland. In 1965, we had our daughter, Bonika Jade Gim. The four of us went to court in 1981 and had our last name Gim legally changed to Chin, our real Chinese last name.

Stan and I moved in 1987 to Marina Village in Alameda, then to Camellia Court in San Leandro in 1997. Stan retired in 1994 with 35 years as a lithographer in the printing industry. After working 22 years at the East Bay Municipal Utility District (a water company in Oakland), I retired in 1999 as an accountant, and we moved to Summerset in Brentwood, followed by a move in 2012 to the Rossmoor Retirement Community in Walnut Creek to live closer to friends and family in the East Bay. We feel like vagabonds, having moved on the average every 12 years. Stan repeats, "This is my last house! I am not moving any more!" While living in Brentwood, I wrote as a senior columnist two articles: "Every Day's a Saturday When You Retire" and "Lost at the Great Wall of China" for the local Contra Costa Times issue of the Antioch Ledger Dispatch.

Stan's mom, Gladys Gim (she resided at the Rose of Sharon Senior Residence since its construction in 1976, as did my mom), lived with dementia in San Leandro for 11 years and was placed in hospice earlier in January, 2014. She has 15 grandchildren and 23 great grandchildren. Sadly, she passed away on September 19, 2014, at an awesome age of 102 years.

Stan and I have four grandchildren. Our son Brandon and his wife Joanna (nee Pang) reside in Danville, CA, and they have a daughter, Nicole Isabelle Chin, age 12. Our daughter Bonnie Zucco in Murrysville (Pittsburgh), PA, has a son, David Michael, age 15, and two daughters, Amy Jade, age 11, and Chloe Ann, age 9. We are proud that they excel in school and love to play musical instruments. Wow, what a family Mom started when she crossed the ocean in 1935. She would be so proud and happy today!!

Made in the USA
San Bernardino, CA
05 June 2015